Translated by Eric McGEER

THE 6th AIRBORNE FROM NORMANDY TO THE BALTIC

PEGASUS 1944

Olivier RICHARD

in collaboration with Paul LE TREVIER

Acknowledgments

It is a pleasure to offer my special thanks to Béatrice Leconte (Boissée), Director of the Pegasus Memorial in Ranville, to the curator, Mark Worthington, to guides Sandrine Cabrol, Nicolas Dumont, and Mathieu Boullé, and to the whole staff at the Pegasus Memorial for their warm welcome and their enthusiastic assistance.

To Eric McGeer, teacher and writer in Toronto, for the quality and precision of his English translation.

I also owe a debt of gratitude to those who generously shared their collections and documents, as well as their knowledge: Olivier Artigues, Kevin Biville, Thierry Chion, Vincent Delamare, Frédéric Guest, F-X Goublet, Pascal Hémery, Jean-François Le Cuziat, Dominique Mulder, Joël Noyon, Geoff Pringle, and Stéphane St-Martin;

Also to Pascaline Dagorn, Director of the Merville Battery Museum, and her helpful staff; and to Mr. Fris Michiels for access to his collection;

To Ludovic and Claude Louis who preserve the memory of the Red Berets at St-Vaast-en-Auge;

To Bern and Fay Robins;

To Jean Migrenne;

And finally, to Francis Dreer and the Big Block Company for their technical assistance.

Olivier Richard
Rouen, April 2015

FOREWORD

by Lieutenant General Sir Hew Pike,
KCB DSO MBE

During the early summer of 1944, the great enterprise to liberate occupied Europe and finally defeat fascism was launched through the beaches of Normandy. D-Day and its aftermath have been the subject of countless histories, relentless analysis and many moving testimonies, as well as films, documentaries and sound recordings. Local and national museums also continue to play a central role in the remembrance of courage and sacrifice, keeping past deeds fresh in our minds and educating new generations in the realities of war. It could even be claimed that museum artefacts and archives provide the most vivid answers to the questions that are foremost in many peoples' thoughts, like "what was it like to be there?" and "how did they overcome the challenges that confronted them?"

The Memorial Pegasus museum exemplifies all that is best in the constant process of learning and remembering, and this new book reflects the manner in which, over the past 70 years, the people of Normandy have continued to pay grateful tribute to their liberators. In this case it is the story of the 6th Airborne Division, a story that is now richly woven into the culture not only of Britain's Parachute Regiment and Airborne Brigade, but into the proud traditions of every regiment that played a part in General Gale's great Division - the 1st Canadian Parachute Battalion, the Oxfordshire and Buckinghamshire Light Infantry (43rd and 52nd), the Royal Ulster Rifles, and the Devonshire Regiment. Also central to the Division's success were the Glider Pilot Regiment and the supporting arms and services, without whom the Division could not have taken to the field.

.../...

I first came to Normandy as a student at the British Army Staff College in 1975, and was spellbound by the "derring-do", modesty and humanity of the accounts given by the likes of John Howard of the "Oxs and Bucks", James Hill commanding 3rd Parachute Brigade, Napier Crookenden the Brigade Major of the 6th Airlanding Brigade and subsequently the CO of 9 PARA, and Alastair Pearson commanding 8 PARA. On that visit, and on many since, I have felt myself constantly touching history, such is the immediacy of events. Equally striking is the way in which our French hosts have continued to make space to hear the call across the years from those who sacrificed their lives in a unique crusade for freedom. When you are in the Commonwealth Cemetery at Ranville, or walking the ground of the battle for Breville, you get the sense that it all happened only a year or two ago. This is remarkable. Especially bearing in mind that the French people lost more civilian casualties to allied bombing in 1944 than the British did throughout the Second World War, this feeling of "time standing still" is a moving tribute to France's commitment to the remembrance of a great common purpose.

This excellent book is a salute to all the veterans who fought in Normandy, so many of whom have continued to support the cause of remembrance over the years. It reflects, too, the importance of the artefacts and documents held by Memorial Pegasus, the "silent witnesses" to so many brave men and women. It brings their call across the years vividly to our minds and into our hearts. We can be moved, too, by the epitaphs in Ranville Cemetery, like that on the headstone of Private ES Corteil of The Parachute Regiment, aged 19:

"Had you known our boy,
You would have loved him too."

Go!

(photo IWM)

6th AIRBORNE DIVISION

3rd PARACHUTE BRIGADE	5th PARACHUTE BRIGADE	6th AIRLANDING BRIGADE
8th (MIDLAND) PARACHUTE BATTALION	7th (LIGHT INFANTRY) PARACHUTE BATTALION	12th BATTALION THE DEVONSHIRE REGIMENT
9th (EASTERN & HOME COUNTIES) PARACHUTE BATTALION	12th (YORKSHIRE) PARACHUTE BATTALION	2nd BATTALION THE OX & BUCKS *
1st CANADIAN PARACHUTE BATTALION	13th (LANCASHIRE) PARACHUTE BATTALION	1st BATTALION THE ROYAL ULSTER RIFLES

Divisional units

22nd Independent Parachute Company (Pathfinders)

ROYAL ENGINEERS
3rd and 591st Parachute Squadron - 249th Field Company
286th Field Park Company

ROYAL ARTILLERY
2nd Forward Observation Unit - 53rd (Worcestershire Yeomanry)
Airlanding Light Regiment - 3rd, 4th and 6th Airlanding Anti-Tank Batteries
2nd Airlanding Anti-Aircraft Battery

6th Airborne Armoured Reconnaissance Regiment (Royal Armoured Corps)

6th Airborne Divisional Signals (Royal Corps of Signals)

ROYAL ARMY MEDICAL CORPS
224th and 225th Parachute Field Ambulances
195th Airlanding Field Ambulance

ROYAL ARMY SERVICE CORPS
716th Light Composite Company
398th and 63rd Composite Company

6th Airborne Division Ordnance Field Park (Royal Army Ordnance Corps)

6th Airborne Division Workshop (Royal Electrical & Mechanical Engineers)

6th Airborne Division Provost Company (Corps of Military Police)

317th Field Security Section (Airborne) Intelligence Corps

* in full, the Oxfordshire & Buckinghamshire Light Infantry

Square insignia on the left: Bellerophon riding the winged steed Pegasus, the emblem worn on the sleeve by members of the British airborne troops. On the right, the cap badge of the Parachute Regiment.

Shoulder title of the Parachute Regiment.

6th Airborne Division

Formations and supporting arms and services

The War Office signed the order authorising the creation of the division on April 23rd, 1943. On May 7th Major-General Richard Gale took command. Although the new airborne unit was only the second of its type in the British Army, it was given the number 6 to fool the Germans into thinking that there was a large number of parachute divisions

The parachute units

In 1940, the first parachute troops were made up of men drawn from No. 2 Commando, but over time their fighting personnel would come from all land forces. To provide a Corps to which all parachute battalions would belong, the Parachute Regiment was created on August 1st, 1942.

The parachute battalions of the 6th Airborne Division were made up of volunteers from infantry regiments who added a wealth of experience and something of their regimental traditions to the parachute units.

■ The 7th (Light Infantry) Parachute Battalion derived from the *10th Battalion, The Somerset Light Infantry.*

■ The 8th (Midland) Parachute Battalion was formed from the *13th Battalion, The Royal Warwickshire Regiment.*

■ The 9th (Eastern & Home Counties) Parachute Battalion came from the *10th Battalion, The Essex Regiment.*

■ The 12th (Yorkshire) Parachute Battalion dipped into the *10th (East Riding) Battalion, The Green Howards,* for its personnel.

■ The 13th (Lancashire) Parachute Battalion was formed by volunteers from the *2nd/4th Battalion, The South Lancashire Regiment.*

■ The 1st Canadian Parachute Battalion was the only parachute formation in the Canadian Army. Established in 1942, it was added to the roster of the 6th Airborne Division in August of 1943 for the duration of the war in Europe.

■ The 22nd Independent Company was a pathfinders unit responsible for reconnaissance and for securing and marking out the landing zones of the parachute troops and gliders. Each airborne division had a company of this type, which came under the overall command of the Parachute Regiment.

Parachute qualification badge worn by Canadian paratroopers.

Cap badge of the 1st Canadian Parachute Battalion.

Cap badge and backing of the 7th Parachute Battalion.

The airborne battalions

Unlike the paratroopers, who volunteered individually, the airborne infantry came from battalions of the land Army which were converted into glider-borne units; however, at the time of the conversion, men preferring to stay in the infantry could ask not to be transferred. As highly trained infantry, the glider-borne men were elite soldiers with the same status as their comrades the paratroopers. They retained the name and insignia of their original regiments.

- The 12th Battalion, the Devonshire Regiment, was employed in coastal defence until 1943 when it was converted into airborne infantry.
- The 2nd Battalion, the Oxfordshire & Buckinghamshire Light Infantry, brought back from India in 1939 and placed in the Airlanding Brigade in 1941.
- The 1st Battalion, the Royal Ulster Rifles, also recalled from India in 1939 and made into an airborne unit in 1941.

Cap badge and shoulder title of the 12th Devonshire Regiment.

Cap badge and shoulder title of the 2nd Oxfordshire & Buckinghamshire Light Infantry.

Cap badge and shoulder title of the 1st Royal Ulster Rifles.

Supporting arms and services

As did every division in the British Army, the 6th Airborne Division had a wide range of supporting arms and services. However, in this particular case, these units took on a very specific character suited to their roles. Furthermore, in contrast with the land army, the airborne divisions did not include a large supporting unit equipped with mortars and machine guns; instead, these weapons were distributed among the platoons within each battalion.

Royal Engineers

Three types of engineering units are to be distinguished within the Airborne Division:

- The 3rd and 591st Parachute Squadrons were attached to the 3rd and 5th Parachute Brigades respectively. The sappers cum paratroopers who made up these units carried out sabotage or demining operations in all situations, including assaults. They also performed the usual functions of the Engineers such as the construction of crossings.
- The 249th Field Company was attached to the 6th Airlanding Brigade with the same duties as the Parachute Squadrons.
- The 286th Field Park Company was attached to divisional headquarters; it looked after workshops, tools and equipment, and specific engine types. On June 6th it brought two bulldozers by gliders to Drop Zone 'N' in order to clear debris and obstacles in preparation for 6th Airlanding Brigade's arrival.

Cap badge and shoulder title of the Royal Engineers.

Cap badges and shoulder title of the Royal Artillery.

Bullion embroidered cap badge of the 53rd Worcestershire Yeomanry.

Royal Artillery

The airborne division had the use of its own artillery. A number of batteries came by glider on the night of June 5th-6th, but the bulk of the units arrived by sea on June 7th.

The artillery in 6th Airborne Division consisted of the following units:

■ The 2nd Forward Observation Unit created on August 1st, 1944. Highly mobile thanks to their jeeps, the Forward Observation Officers sought out enemy targets and brought down supporting fire by radio.

■ The 53rd (Worcestershire Yeomanry) Airlanding Light Regiment was descended from a very old unit. Designated an airborne unit in 1943, it constituted the heaviest artillery support in 6th Airborne Division. It included three batteries of eight fieldpieces each, these being the 75 mm Pack Howitzers of American make.

■ The 3rd and 4th Airlanding Anti-tank Batteries were attached to the two Parachute Brigades. The three battalions of the Airlanding Brigade had their own anti-tank guns in the form of six 6-pounder in each of their support companies. The Airlanding Anti-Tank Batteries were divided into four 'Troops' equipped with four guns each, for a total of twelve 6-pounders and four powerful 17-pounders. In January of 1945, a new battery (the 6th) was formed to protect the divisional service units.

■ The 2nd Airlanding Light Anti-Aircraft Battery was created in May of 1943. This light air defence unit was equipped with eighteen 40 mm Bofors guns and forty-eight 20 mm Hispano-Suiza guns.

6th A.A.R.R.

■ The 6th Airborne Armoured Reconnaissance Regiment was an armoured unit employed in a reconnaissance role. It dated from 1942. The 6th Airborne Division was the only one to have such a regiment which consisted of a reconnaissance squadron (with jeeps, scout cars, motorcycles and Bren carriers), a support squadron (with mortars and machine guns), and an armoured squadron equipped with light Tetrarch tanks. On August 6th, 1944, 'A' Squadron would receive eight Cromwell tanks. The tank crews were made up of men trained in the Royal Armoured Corps or other armoured units.

Royal Corps of Signals

The 6th Airborne Division comprised a headquarter company of the Royal Corps of Signals and three signals companies:

■ No.1 Company was attached to Division Headquarters to take charge of its communications.

■ No.2 Company established communication links between Brigade Headquarters and those of the artillery, engineers, and reconnaissance regiments. It was responsible for maintaining the lines of communication between the field and the various levels of command in the division.

■ No.3 Company organised communications at the division's base headquarters in Great Britain.

Cap badge and shoulder title worn by the 6th A.A.R.R..

Cap badge and shoulder title of the Royal Corps of Signal.

Royal Army Medical Corps

■ The 224th and 225th Parachute Field Ambulances were attached to the 3rd and 5th Parachute Brigades respectively.

■ The 195th Airlanding Field Ambulance was made part of 6th Airlanding Brigade. Each of these Field Ambulances included nine officers and a hundred other ranks. These units consisted of a headquarters, two surgical teams, four treatment sections (triage and evacuation). Medical and surgical equipment was dropped in containers or brought by glider. In addition, each battalion had the services of a medical officer and a medical platoon.

Royal Army Service Corps

The airborne RASC was responsible for resupply in foodstuffs and munitions.

■ The 398th and 63rd Composite Companies saw to the refilling of supply containers and Wicker Panniers in Great Britain. It was also their trucks that conveyed supplies to the airfields and their companies that undertook to carry and drop these supplies.

■ The 716th Light Composite Company included three airborne platoons and one parachute platoon. They were equipped with jeeps and trailers loaded with provisions, munitions, and all manner of materiel to set up supply depots after the airborne landings. This unit operated directly in the drop zones and landing zones to gather reserve supplies and give them out to the different units.

Royal Army Ordnance Corps

■ Nearly eighty drivers and storesmen from the ordnance corps, half of them breveted as paratroopers, the other half trained as glider-borne troops, served in the 6th Airborne Division Ordnance Field Park. They tended to the maintenance of the division's equipment and made use of trucks, jeeps, and trailers loaded with spare parts of all kinds (weapons, radios, motors, etc.). Their stores were usually side by side with the workshops of the Royal Electrical & Mechanical Engineers (R.E.M.E.).

Royal Electrical & Mechanical Engineers

■ The tradesmen of the 6th Airborne Division Workshop looked after the maintenance and repair of weapons and vehicles. While on operations, an Advanced Workshop Detachment was deployed with the forward troops. Some of the personnel was parachuted in, while the rest arrived in three Horsa gliders, each one containing four men and a jeep with a trailer loaded with materiel. One of the jeeps carried a generator, the second radio maintenance equipment, and the third the tools and parts. Other Light Aid Detachments were assigned to each brigade, to the engineers, artillery, signals, and the reconnaissance regiment.

Corps of Military Police

■ The 6th Airborne Division Provost Company was responsible for keeping a close watch on the camps and airfields before major operations began. The provost corps made sure that troop concentration areas were hermetically sealed so that no information leaked out. Subsequently, when in the field, the Military Police were supposed to keep soldiers going in the right direction after their landing, ensure the security of divisional command posts, take custody of prisoners, and mark out routes.

Intelligence Corps

■ The 317th Field Security Section (Airborne) was responsible for intelligence and counter-espionage in the division. In the six months leading up to D-Day, this section oversaw the security and secrecy of 6th Airborne Division's transit camps. This unit was made up of one officer and seventeen Non Commissioned Officers (NCOs), most of them fluent in several languages. On operations, they were the ones who interrogated the prisoners of war and collected informations about ennemy forces.

Royal Army Chaplain's Department

■ An Anglican chaplain accompanied each battalion. He took care of religious services and offered a reassuring, comforting presence to the soldiers, both at base and on operations. On the frontline, the chaplain shared the soldiers' existence, tending to the wounded and sending news to their families. He was also responsible for recovering the papers and personal effects of the men killed, and overseeing the identification and burial of the dead. Catholic and Jewish chaplains were also available, the former at the divisional level, the latter at the army corps level.

Glider Pilot Regiment (Army Air Corps)

■ The Glider Pilot Regiment and the Parachute Regiment were subordinate to the Army Air Corps which administered the air arm of the ground forces. Glider pilots wore distinctive qualification wings and cap badge but sported the flash particular to their regiment. Recruited from the army beginning with the rank of sergeant, they took the training course common to all RAF pilots, followed by special instruction to qualify as glider pilots. At the same time they were trained soldiers perfectly capable of fighting on the ground if circumstances dictated.

Cap badge and shoulder title of the Royal Army Medical Corps

Cap badge and shoulder title of the Corps of Military Police

Cap badge and shoulder title of the Royal Army Service Corps

Cap badge and shoulder title of the Intelligence Corps

Cap badge and shoulder title of the Royal Army Ordnance Corps

Cap badge and shoulder title of the Royal Army Chaplain's Department

Cap badge and shoulder title of the Royal Electrical & Mechanical Engineers

Cap badge and shoulder title of the Glider Pilot Regiment

Euston II, the bridge over the Orne at Ranville. (photo © IWM)

Operation Deadstick: the capture of the bridges at Bénouville and Ranville

The capture of the bridges over the Orne River and the Caen Canal, and their defence against all attempts to recapture them, was one of the principal objectives of 6th Airborne Division. The capture of these bridges required the use a unit specially created and trained for the task. The establishment of a defensive perimeter around the zone embracing the bridges would fall to 5th Parachute Brigade.

Above: the wreckage of one of the three Horsas that landed by Pegasus Bridge. Below: two of the gliders that carried the assault force to Pegasus Bridge; the line of trees hides the canal and the drawbridge. (photos © IWM)

Under the command of Major John Howard, the force slated for Operation Deadstick was made up of 'D' Company of the 2nd Oxfordshire & Buckinghamshire Light Infantry, reinforced by two platoons from 'B' Company (under Lieutenants Sandy Smith and Dennis Fox) and thirty sappers (detached from the 249th Field Company) commanded by Captain Jock Neilson. The reliance on glider-borne troops was imposed on General Gale because of the precision and the relative discretion of their landing. Had the same number of paratroopers been used, they would have been scattered during the night drop and their reassembly after landing would have used up precious time.

The Orne River was the opening scene for the greatest invasion in history.

Since April, Howard had been training his men near Exeter, on bridges very much like the ones at Bénouville and Ranville. To seize control of the structures before the Germans could blow them up, the attackers had to take maximum advantage of the brief effect of surprise caused by their arrival. The demolition charges would be dismantled by Captain Neilson's sappers. The 169 men in the assault force would be transported in six Horsa gliders split into two groups of three, heading for two small Landing Zones – LZ X at the bridge spanning the canal (code named Euston I), and LZ Y at the Ranville bridge (Euston II). In both cases, the gliders would have to land right by the bridges in a very narrow strip of ground between the two waterways while avoiding the marshes and embankments. Like the men they were carrying, the glider pilots had undergone intensive training, endlessly repeating each phase of the approach and landing. Each of the six crews was on its own and had to find its own way once released by the tow plane. The pilots had to steer by compass and chronometer, all while trying to spot landmarks below in the darkness...

Towed by Halifaxes from 298 and 644 Squadrons, the six Horsas, overloaded with men and equipment, took off from Tarrant Rushton a little before 23h00 on June 5th. After flying over the Channel without incident, the gliders numbered 91, 92, and 93 were released close to their objective at Euston I, the bridge over the Caen Canal. At the end of a remarkably accurate course, Glider 91, piloted by Staff Sergeants J.H. Wallwork and J. Ainsworth, came to a stop with its nose in barbed wire, just fifty meters from the bridge. The cockpit disintegrated under the shock and the two pilots were wounded when thrown out. In a few seconds the airborne soldiers sorted themselves out from the commotion following the landing and made for their objectives in total silence. Amazingly, the Germans were not alerted by the racket; the only surviving sentinel, Helmut Römer, would say later that he thought that a bomber had crashed.

Operation Deadstick, the capture of the bridges

Glider 92, guided by Staff-Sergeants P. Hobbs and O. Bolland, came to rest not far from 91. Its cockpit too was destroyed and Hobbs received severe lacerations to his legs. The third Horsa, Glider 93 with Staff-Sergeant G. Barkway and Sergeant P. Boyle at the controls, broke apart on coming to a stop. One of its passengers, Lance Corporal Fred Greenhalgh, was flung out and drowned in the swamp. In the meantime, Lieutenant H.D. Brotheridge and his No. 1 Platoon reached the bridge. A German fired off a flare before being killed by the lieutenant who then ran to the western edge of the bridge where he silenced a machine gun post with a grenade. In the course of this action he was mortally wounded by a bullet in the neck. Following his lead, his men crossed the bridge firing with all their weapons and eliminated the German defences. On the far bank, No. 2 Platoon under Lieutenant David Wood overran the enemy dugouts and a 50 mm gun. Lieutenant Smith's No. 3 Platoon crossed the bridge in turn to give support to No. 1 Platoon on the west bank, while Neilson's sappers determined that the charges needed to blow up the structure were not in place.

In LZ Y, near the bridge at Ranville, Gliders 95 (steered by Staff-Sergeants S. Parson and L. Guthrie) and 96 (Staff-Sergeants R. Howard and F. Baacke) came to earth without trouble; however, there was quite a drawback to reckon with, in that Glider 94 under Staff-Sergeants A. Lawrence and H. Shorter, was missing. In addition to the platoon led by Lieutenant Tony Hooper, this glider carried Captain Brian Priday who was second in command of the assault force (codenamed "Coup de main Party"). Unfortunately, the pilot of the Halifax towing Glider 94 had mistaken the Orne with the Dives River, and it was near this latter waterway where Lawrence and Shorter had set down their craft. After many an adventure and tight scrape, the whole group managed to rejoin 'D' Company towards 02h30 on June 8th. Even though bereft of a third of its men, the assault force ordered to capture Euston II accomplished its mission without encountering serious opposition. The main source of resistance was an MG 34 which was immediately knocked out by a 2" mortar. Soon enough Corporal Tappenden, 'D' Company's radio operator, was sending the signal "Ham and Jam" confirming that the two bridges had been captured intact. A mere fifteen minutes had elapsed since the first glider landed...

Shortly after midnight, when the gliders of the "Coup de main Party" were approaching their objectives, pathfinders from the 22nd Independent Parachute Company were likewise touching down on the soil of Normandy. Jumping with them were a certain number of advance units of the parachute battalions still to come. Last but not least, one of the figures in this vanguard was Brigadier Nigel

Three men from Horsa no. 94, from left to right: Private Frank Gardner (killed in Germany in March 1945); Captain Brian Priday; and Lance Corporal William Lambley (killed in Holland in February 1945). (photo © IWM)

Poett himself, the commander of 5th Parachute Brigade. After landing in DZ N, Brigadier Poett let himself be guided to the bridges by the sound of the fighting and, once assured that the operation had been a success, went to congratulate Howard who was more than a little surprised by his arrival. At 00h50 the full complement of 5th Parachute Brigade jumped – in less than half an hour, 129 aircraft dropped 2,026 men and 702 containers over an area which, alas, greatly exceeded the limits of DZ N. There were many reasons for this dispersion: chief among them were poor visibility which did not allow for identification of landmarks on the ground, and a high wind that scattered the sticks and several markers placed too far to the east.

If the paratroopers did their best to regroup, many of the containers could not be located during the night and their contents (mortars, machine guns, radios) would be sorely missed when the Germans counterattacked in the morning. Around Euston I and II, the Ox and Bucks handily repelled the enemy attacks. At 01h30, several German self-propelled gun approaching from the west attempted to push through to the bridges, but when Sergeant Thornton destroyed the lead armoured vehicle with a PIAT gun (Projectile, Infantry, Anti-Tank), the others pulled back. The 7th Battalion which should have been on its way to reinforce Howard's men was widely dispersed and more than half its men were wandering around in the swamp to the east.

Lieutenant-Colonel Richard Pine-Coffin and his paratroopers reached the bridges at 02h30 and took up positions on the west bank at Bénouville and Le Port. For twelve hours, without their heavy weapons, they would stand off every enemy attack without giving an inch. The 12th Parachute Battalion was also widely dispersed. Reduced to two thirds of its strength, it took up its position towards 04h00 at Bas-de-Ranville. There, under fire from enemy mortars and artillery, it drove back two attacks by the 125th Panzergrenadier Regiment aimed at Ranville. Less dispersed, the 13th Parachute Battalion carried out its assignments quickly; between 03h00 and 04h00 Ranville fell into its hands, while at 03h20 the seventy-two gliders of Operation Tonga descended on LZ N which had been cleared of the obstacles known as *"Rommel's asparagus"* by 'A' Company of the 13th Battalion. A good deal of the divisional artillery came in these gliders, along with elements of the Royal Engineers, the Royal Army Service Corps, and General Gale himself. The commander of the 6th Airborne was now on the ground, in person, together with his men.

John Howard with the snipers of his company at the Chateau St-Côme in mid July 1944: Left to right, Private "Wackers" Waite, Private "Pete" Musty, Private "Nobby" Clarke, Major Howard, Private "Rocky" Bright, Private "Paddy" O'Donnell, Private "Eddy" Edwards. (D.R. Mémorial Pegasus).

John Howard at Bénouville on June 5th, 1990.

Major Howard before the landings. This portrait inspired the bronze bust placed on the bank of the Caen Canal, at the very spot where Staff-Sergeant Jim Wallwork landed his Horsa glider. (photo © IWM)

Exit hole left by the bullet that passed through Major's helmet.

The bust of Major Howard on the spot where he landed on June 6th, 1944.

The impact of the bullet that struck the front of his helmet.

Major John Howard
DSO, Croix de Guerre

A legendary character in the story of D-Day and an inspiring leader, the man who conducted the assault on the bridges at Bénouville and Ranville presented an unusual profile for an officer up from the ranks. In an England where social origins meant a great deal, the rigour and determination with which John Howard pursued his military career and his own destiny enabled him to overcome many hurdles.

Born in London on December 8th, 1912, in a modest household in the West End, John Howard was the eldest of nine brothers and sisters. He was an excellent student who nevertheless had to go to work from the age of fourteen since his family could not afford to pay for his schooling. While employed in clerical work, he shared his free time between Scouting, which allowed him to satisfy his appetite for sports, and night courses which he took in order to improve his lot in life. Left jobless by the financial crisis in 1929, he enlisted in the army and joined the King's Shropshire Light Infantry. Lost and unhappy at first among rather coarse companions, his sporting prowess enabled him to find his bearings and become an instructor in physical education. In 1936 Corporal Howard met Joy, a young woman from a higher social station than his own who feared her mother's disapproval. Against all expectation she accepted John and they were married in 1939. The same year Howard came to the end of his enlistment term and became a policeman in Oxford. After Britain mobilised he returned to the King's Shropshire Light Infantry and his former rank of corporal, but the war tended to hasten promotion and Howard rose through the ranks until he became Regimental Sergeant-Major in April of 1940. As circumstances now allowed men risen from the ranks to become officers, Howard straightway obtained his commission. Assigned to the 2nd Battalion of the Oxfordshire & Buckinghamshire Light Infantry, he was at first shunned by the other officers; however, his capacity for command won him acceptance, but not before a few difficult weeks had gone by. In 1941 he took command of a company after being promoted to captain. At the end of the year, the Ox & Bucks was slated for conversion into airborne infantry as part of the 1st Airlanding Brigade. In the course of this transformation Howard accepted a reduction in rank to lieutenant without batting an eye. He soon returned to his rank and then became a major in May of 1942. Deeply attached to his company, a great many of whom were Londoners, he made them into a remarkable instrument of war, leading his men in person on the most gruelling exercises. The high standard of 'D' Company earned its selection as the unit to carry out the assault on the bridges over the Orne River. On June 7th Howard was targeted by a sniper. The bullet passed through his helmet and creased his scalp without doing any further damage. By the end of the Normandy campaign, the surviving members of 'D' Company were truly devoted to their commander, but unfortunately, it so happened that he would no longer lead them in battle. On November 13th, 1944, Howard was involved in a head-on collision with an American truck. Both legs, his left knee, and his right hip were broken. In March of 1945, he too soon resumed training in order to rejoin his unit, and the severe complications were enough to cause him to finish the war in the hospital and then to be invalided out of the service. Over the years, on each June 6th, Howard and the veterans of the assault would gather together at Pegasus Bridge, raising their glasses without fail at 00h16 in memory of their "Fallen Comrades."

The Mark I Airborne helmet with leather chinstrap used by paratroopers after July 1942. The one shown, marked on either side with the flash of the 2nd Ox & Bucks, was worn by Major Howard in Normandy. The scars left by the bullet that struck the helmet on June 7th are not visible here.

Mementoes of Major Howard

A few of this officer's personal effects remain on the very site where he and his men carried out their famous "coup de main." Over the years, Major Howard and his next of kin offered these remarkable items for display at the Pegasus Memorial. These historic artefacts, connected to one of the most significant events of the Second World War, also help to recall the daily life of a frontline soldier, as well as a number of traits among the officers of the Ox & Bucks.

This shoulder flash, worn by the 52nd Ox & Bucks in 1942, was still sported by Major Howard in 1944. He was one of the "intractables" who preferred it to the new flash with "Oxf. & Bucks."

Major Howard's medals, from left to right: Distinguished Service Order, 1939-45 Star, France-Germany Star, Defence Medal, 1939-45 Medal, and the French Croix de Guerre with Palm.

John Howard's survival kit. Most men of the 6th Airborne were provided with these for the invasion. At left, needle and thread. Above, water pouch and emergency rations.

Major Howard's escape compass. These miniature compasses, easily concealed on the person, were widely distributed among the Airborne units.

The beret worn by Major Howard during the Second World War. The small cap badge (magnified in the inset) was in fact the insignia worn on the collar; the practice of attaching it to the beret was adopted by the battalion's officers.

One of Jim Wallwork's original shoulder titles.

The veteran's cap badge that belonged to Jim Wallwork. In the 1950s this type replaced the one worn by the Army Air Corps during the war.

Four assaults at the controls of a glider

Staff-Sergeant Wallwork

Born in Salford in 1919, James Harley "Jim" Wallwork joined the Glider Pilot Regiment in 1942. Famous for his brilliant work in piloting the first glider to land in Normandy on D-Day, an exploit that earned him the Distinguished Flying Medal, he was one of the rare British glider pilots to have made it through four large-scale airborne assaults. On July 9th, 1943, when the invasion of Sicily began, he was one of very few who managed to land safely on solid ground. After recovering from the wounds sustained on D-Day, he took the controls of a Horsa on September 17th for Operation Market Garden; six months later he steered a Hamilcar to the far bank of the Rhine in Operation Varsity. An emigrant to Canada in 1957, Jim Wallwork never flew in civil aviation and his feats as a glider pilot remained the stuff of military lore.

Above: Jim Wallwork before D-Day. Opposite: Wearing his veteran's blazer of the Glider Pilot Regiment.

Jim Wallwork's medals, donated to the Pegasus Memorial. Left to right, the Distinguished Flying Medal, 1939-45 Star, Africa Star, Italy Star, France-Germany Star, Defence Medal, 1939-45 Medal, and Efficiency Medal.

Wallwork's glider in Landing Zone X.
(photo © IWM)

Glider pilot's qualification wings worn by Jim Wallwork.

Glider pilot's helmet, the type used after 1943. It combines the RAF flying helmet with a protective shell made of fibreglass. The model here shows the full ensemble worn in flight, with the Mark VIII goggles and oxygen mask which without the tube had no respiratory use; it served instead as a microphone.

During a visit to the Pegasus Memorial, Jim Wallwork inscribed his glider's registration number (PF 800) and his signature on the shell of his helmet.

Connection plug for the on-board radio.

Geoff Barkway's decorations: On the left is the Distinguished Flying Medal, awarded for "the accomplishment of his task with great precision, skill, and courage." It was some time before he received the medal, however, owing to a mix-up in names.

Geoff Barkway kept these three pieces of plywood from his Horsa glider, symbolic relics from the site of the assault.

Barkway in 1944. Enlisting at age 17 in 1939, he was 20 when he volunteered to serve as a glider pilot.

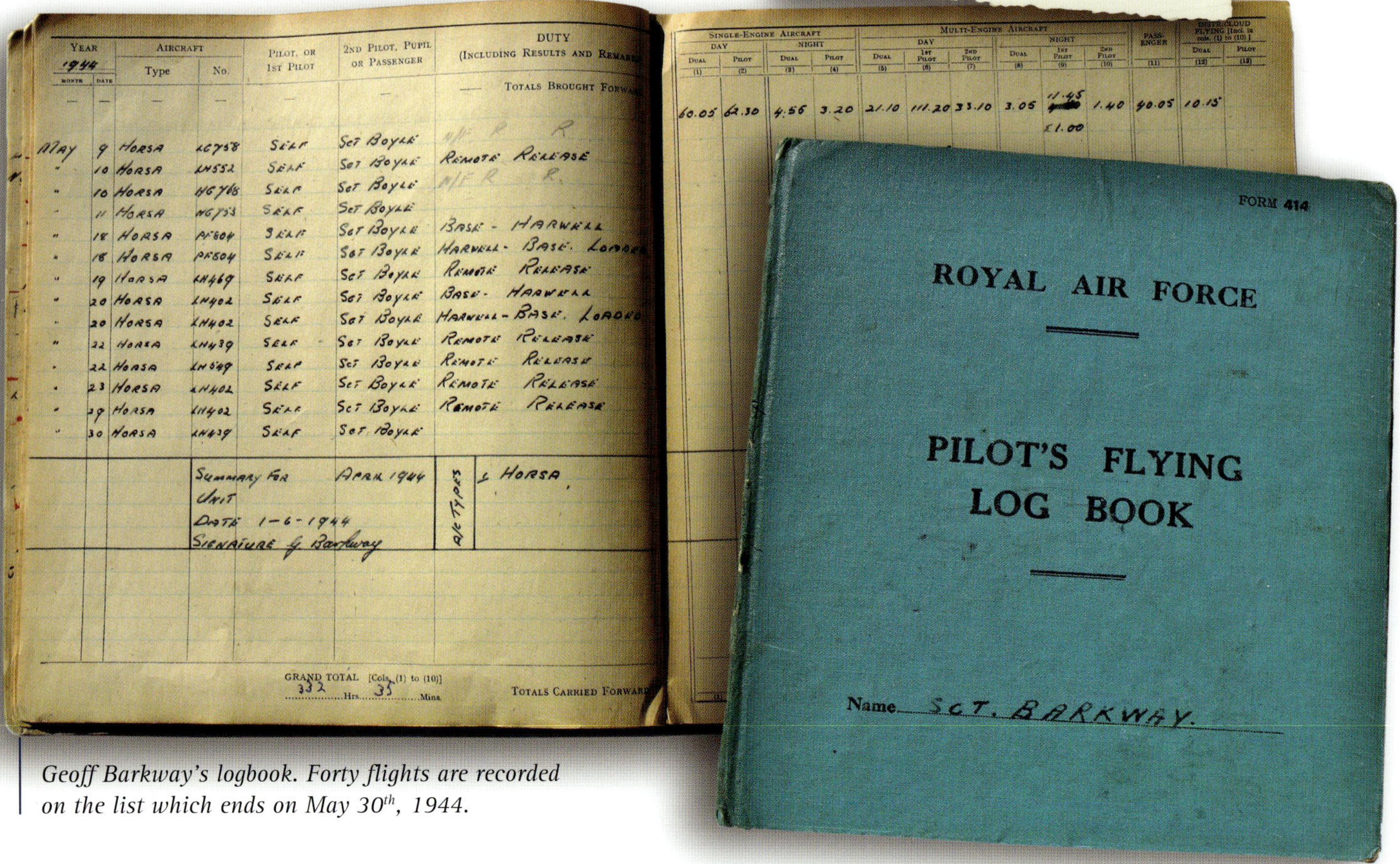

Geoff Barkway's logbook. Forty flights are recorded on the list which ends on May 30th, 1944.

The pilots of Horsa no. 93 on a pilgrimage to the site of their landing. At left, Geoff Barkway, and Peter Boyle.

Staff-Sergeant
Geoffrey Sidney Barkway, DFM

© The objects shown on these pages come from the collections of the Pegasus Memorial in Ranville.

Released at 5,800 feet, Horsa no. 93 commenced its descent through the clouds. At the controls, Geoff Barkway, a twenty-two year old Londoner, picked out bit by bit a forest here, two waterways there... Meanwhile, Peter Boyle, his co-pilot, advised him of the timing and course with the aid of a chronometer and compass. The heavily laden glider came in very quickly and shot past No. 92. The braking parachute was not used and the craft came to a stop while shattering at the front. The two pilots got out and carried ammunition to the bridge; then Barkway was hit. His right arm, practically severed, later had to be amputated.

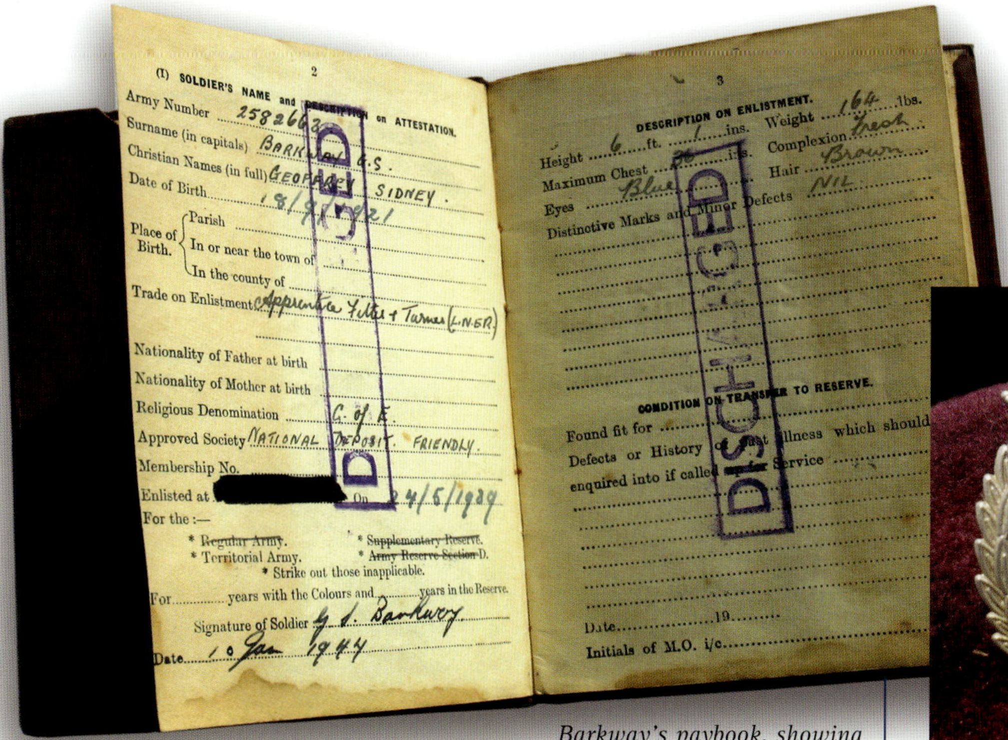

2

(I) SOLDIER'S NAME and DESCRIPTION on ATTESTATION.

Army Number 2582663
Surname (in capitals) BARKWAY G.S.
Christian Names (in full) GEOFFREY SIDNEY.
Date of Birth 18/9/1921
Place of Birth. Parish
In or near the town of
In the county of
Trade on Enlistment Apprentice Fitter + Turner (L.N.E.R.)
Nationality of Father at birth
Nationality of Mother at birth
Religious Denomination C. of E.
Approved Society NATIONAL DEPOSIT. FRIENDLY.
Membership No.
Enlisted at [redacted] On 24/5/1939
For the :—
* ~~Regular Army.~~ * ~~Supplementary Reserve.~~
* Territorial Army. * ~~Army Reserve Section D.~~
* Strike out those inapplicable.
For .... years with the Colours and .... years in the Reserve.
Signature of Soldier G. S. Barkway
Date 10 Jan 1944

DISCHARGED

3

DESCRIPTION ON ENLISTMENT.

Height 6 ft. 1 ins. Weight 164 lbs.
Maximum Chest 36 ins. Complexion Fresh
Eyes Blue Hair Brown
Distinctive Marks and Minor Defects NIL

CONDITION ON TRANSFER TO RESERVE.

Found fit for
Defects or History of past illness which should be enquired into if called up for Service

Date .... 19........
Initials of M.O. i/c ....

DISCHARGED

Barkway's paybook, showing the demobilisation stamp.

Cap badge of the Army Air Corps worn by Geoff Barkway.

Lieutenant Den Brotheridge

Like Major Howard, Herbert Denham Brotheridge was an officer who came up from the ranks, something that brought the two men together. He commanded no. 25 Platoon in 'D' Company which arrived in the first Horsa (no. 91) at Bénouville. On the bridge, his soldiers saw him throw a grenade into a machine gun nest before crumpling up with a bullet through his neck. The lieutenant's flask, engraved with his name and serial number, is conserved at the Memorial, not far from the bridge which he helped to capture.

The flask carried by Den Brotheridge. Below, his portrait.

Three men, three fates

Three men from the Ox & Bucks. Two would share the sad distinction of being the first Allied soldiers to die in Normandy on June 6th, 1944. The third, already a veteran of other campaigns, would serve with honour throughout the days he spent at the front. Although wounded, he would survive the war. Precious relics summon up the memory of these men at the Pegasus Memorial.

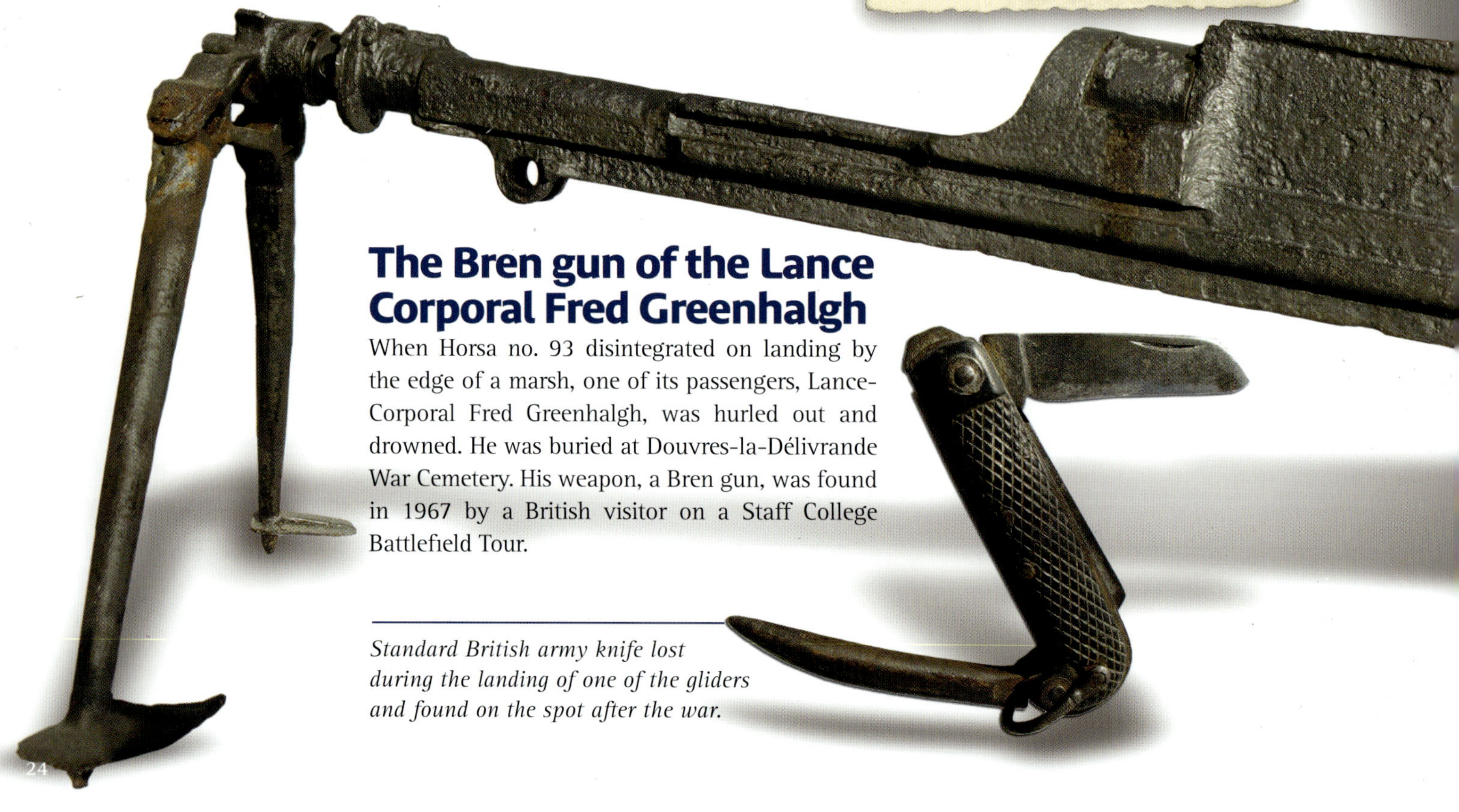

The Bren gun of the Lance Corporal Fred Greenhalgh

When Horsa no. 93 disintegrated on landing by the edge of a marsh, one of its passengers, Lance-Corporal Fred Greenhalgh, was hurled out and drowned. He was buried at Douvres-la-Délivrande War Cemetery. His weapon, a Bren gun, was found in 1967 by a British visitor on a Staff College Battlefield Tour.

Standard British army knife lost during the landing of one of the gliders and found on the spot after the war.

Sergeant Charles « Wagger » Thornton, MM

This battle-hardened, efficient NCO, a qualified paratrooper, had already served in North Africa and Italy. In Operation Deadstick on June 6th, 1944, he was part of the group drawn from 'B' Company under Lieutenant Dennis Fox. He arrived in Landing Zone Y on board Horsa no. 96, and following the capture of Ranville he volunteered to make contact with the paratroopers of the 7th Battalion. During a patrol he used a PIAT to destroy a German self-propelled gun whose ammunition exploded with spectacular effect. The other vehicles drew back, putting an end to a possible counterattack on the bridges. The next day, he led 'B' Company during the capture of Escoville. Wounded in an action at Hérouvillette, he nevertheless manned an observation post until the very end of the battle. For all his gallant actions he received the Military Medal.

Sergeant Thornton's battle dress.

"Wagger" Thornton at a D-Day commemoration.

© The objects shown on these pages come from the collections of the Pegasus Memorial in Ranville.

The army number of an unknown soldier who left his helmet in Normandy.

Someone living in Ranville kept this helmet from the 2nd Ox & Bucks. Even if we do not know the circumstances of its being left behind, we can be sure from the army number that it did not belong to a soldier who was killed in battle.

Relics of the 6th Airborne at Bénouville et Ranville

Several of these relics of the 6th Airborne were preserved as souvenirs, while others, in more pragmatic fashion, were recycled by the local population hard pressed from the effects of the fighting. More than a few items that figured prominently in the first hours of D-Day found entirely new uses, often remote from their originally intended function.

Supplies essential to the Red Berets were dropped by parachute in metal containers or in Wicker Panniers. This one was found at Ranville. The metal panels on the sides indicate that it carried 146 pounds of supplies for the Royal Engineers.

This is the upper portion of the door of one of the Horsas that landed near the bridge at Bénouville. Retrieved by an inhabitant of the village, it was sawn apart and had its plexiglass removed; it then rendered valuable service for many years as the door to a henhouse, the poultry using the opening to go in and out.

On the inside are the hatches that were opened in the first minutes of June 6th, 1944.

Bits of the labels showing the proper placement of equipment loaded in the fuselage.

This piece of the tail flap from a Horsa glider was retrieved from the same henhouse in Bénouville. The painted canvas has stood up well against the ravages of time and chickens...

A US press photograph from 1945 showing British trucks rolling over Pegasus Bridge.

An enduring symbol of D-Day
Pegasus Bridge

This drawbridge (known as the Scherzer type, after the 19th-century American engineer William Scherzer) was installed in 1935 to replace a swing bridge dating from 1857. After being lengthened in 1964, the bridge was replaced thirty years later by a larger model.
The original bridge, a moving and enduring remnant, has ever since been on display at the Pegasus Memorial, close by its former location.

Two veterans from 'C' Company in 1990. Ted Tappenden, the radio operator who sent the signal "Ham and Jam," and below, Wally Parr.

The original Pegasus Bridge shortly before it was replaced in 1994.

The memorial panel being made soon after the landings; note the crosses awaiting use.

The original panel now conserved in the Pegasus Memorial.

In the park adjoining the Pegasus Memorial, the bridge has once more become a place of pilgrimage.

Men gave their lives to capture this bridge, the armies that used it went on to liberate Europe. The original bridge on site at the Memorial, in a setting well suited to visitors. In the foreground is the plaque honouring the memory of Lieutenant Brotheridge.

The open-air replica of the Horsa at the Memorial offers visitors a remarkable view of the glider in its 1944 version.

Gliders and tow planes

The better part of 6th Airborne's troops and equipment arrived by glider in the course of two distinct operations. On the night of June 5th-6th, between midnight and 04h00, ninety-eight gliders landed as part of Operation Tonga. Some carried the assault forces, others the heavy equipment which the paratroopers would need, as well as the divisional headquarters.

From 21h00 on, during Operation Mallard, 256 gliders would convey the rest of the Airlanding Brigade (the 12th Devonshire, minus 'A' company, arrived by sea on June 7th), along with its supporting units.

The Horsa glider

Nearly 5,000 of these gliders were produced by Airspeed Ltd. between 1942 and 1945. The ones used on D-Day were the Mark I types. The Mark II, equipped with a hinged nose, came into service in the summer of 1944 and was to be used by the 6th Airborne only in Operation Varsity. The Horsa had a wooden framework covered with plywood and coated canvas. It was twenty metres in length with a wingspan of twenty-seven metres. Two men did the piloting. The Horsa could carry a

A rehearsal in April 1944 demonstrating the proper technique for loading a jeep onto a Horsa glider.
(photo © IWM)

These Hamilcar gliders freshly coated with their "invasion stripes," await departure for Normandy. (photo PAC)

Loading a Bren carrier on board a Hamilcar for Operation Varsity. (photo PAC)

varied load. It normally had room for twenty-five fully equipped soldiers, but when necessary, more than thirty men could fit in. It could also carry a jeep towing a trailer, a wheeled gun (either a 6-pounder anti-tank gun or a 20 mm anti-aircraft gun), or a motorcycle. Heavy equipment could be loaded through a side door set behind the cockpit. After the Horsa had landed, removable bolts made it possible to unhinge the rear section and open the fuselage for the rapid unloading of men and equipment.

The Hamilcar glider

This large craft, twenty metres long with a wingspan of over thirty-three metres, was the brainchild of General Aircraft Ltd. They were built by the Railway Carriage & Wagon Company in Birmingham which produced 412 Hamilcars between 1941 and 1945. Piloted by two men, it could carry up to eight tons of equipment, which might include a light Tetrarch tank, or two Universal Carriers, or two Dingo Scout Cars, or a 17-pounder gun with its Morris C8 tractor. The Hamilcar was loaded from the front once the hinged nose section had been swung open.

The reader will recognise the Horsa's access ramps used to board the jeep in the photo shown on the opposite page.

The tow planes — "Tugs"

■ The Armstrong Whitworth Albemarle was a twin-engine medium bomber brought into service as a transport aircraft in 1941. It was used for reconnaissance, transporting paratroopers (ten in all), resupply, or towing gliders. It had a range of nearly 2,000 kilometres (without glider). The paratroopers jumped through a hatch in the floor at the rear of the fuselage.

■ The Handley Page Halifax was a four-engine heavy bomber introduced in 1941. Quickly supplanted by the Lancaster for bombing operations, it was then reassigned to reconnaissance and transport roles. Used mainly as a "Tug," this powerful aircraft was one of two models capable of towing a fully loaded Hamilcar.

■ The Short Stirling was also a four-engined heavy bomber which was employed as a tow plane for the Horsa and the Hamilcar. It could also carry twenty-four paratroopers, or deliver its conventional load of forty men, two jeeps, or a single jeep towing a tractor or a 6-pounder gun. Its range of operation was 3,750 kilometres.

■ The famous Douglas C-47 "Skytrain" ou "Dakota" was an American twin-engine transport adopted by the RAF in 1942. It could serve equally well as a transport for paratroopers or as a tow plane for gliders. It could carry twenty-eight fully equipped paratroopers who left the aircraft through a large side door much more convenient than the rear hatch in the Albermarle.

Souvenirs of a D-Day Horsa. The cockade (or roundel) from the fuselage and a part of the stabiliser.

What happened to the gliders after D-Day?

318 Horsas and 34 Hamilcars were involved in Operations Tonga and Mallard. With a view to subsequent operations, the British set out to recover a number of these gliders. In August of 1944, a workshop was created at St-Aubin d'Arquenay and forty refitted aircraft were able to make the return trip to England – aside from one that crashed on take-off, all made it back in one piece. A good many canopies had to be completed with plywood since the local population had scavenged some plexiglass from the wrecks. Over a thousand tons of spare parts and a certain number of intact tail sections went back by boat.

The view from the cockpit of the model Horsa at the Pegasus Memorial.

Detail of the Horsa's covering, painted canvas glued to a plywood surface.

One of the removable parts that allowed the rear section of the Horsa to be swung open to unload vehicles.

Interior of an authentic cabin section from a Horsa glider, now on display at the Pegasus Memorial. No other section of this size exists anywhere else in the world.

An identical cabin photographed in 1944, showing men of the 2nd Ox & Bucks with their unit flashes on both sides of their helmets. (photo © IWM)

Front wheel of a Horsa.

An example of post-war recycling. This bench from a Horsa glider did further service as a park bench in Normandy until the 1990s.

This valve in a Hamilcar glider allowed the exhaust fumes from a tank to escape while the vehicle was idling before the landing. Some of the instructions for its use can still be read.

Switch for the identification and navigation lights on a Horsa glider, with a toggle switch for each light and a key for sending identification signals in Morse code.

The glider's tow cable. A telephone line inside the plait allowed communication with the tow plane.

The controls for releasing the tow rope on a Hamilcar glider.

This beam found at Ranville came from a Hamilcar glider

Bottles such as the one shown supplied compressed air for operating the wing flaps and the braking system in gliders. Retrieved by soldiers and civilians, they went on to a new career far from their original purpose. Four of them are still to be seen in the war cemetery at Ranville, made into borders for the Cross put up in September 1944 by sappers from the 6th Airborne Division. Another, on display at the Pegasus Memorial, was used as a bell after the destruction of the church in Bréville.

A member of the Royal Army Service Corps with the 6th Airborne before the monument in the Ranville cemetery; the compressed air bottles are perfectly visible.
(D.R. Mémorial Pegasus)

This compass was shaken free in the cockpit of a Horsa glider that finished its flight in a garden in Ranville.

The "joystick" or steering wheel of a Hamilcar glider.

In the summer of 1944, a young inhabitant of Merville-Franceville found these insignia on an abandoned battle dress blouse.

The guns of Merville:
The 9th Battalion's feat of arms

In the early hours of June 6th, under the command of Lieutenant-Colonel Terence Otway, the paratroopers of the 9th Battalion and the sappers of the 591st Squadron (Royal Engineers) faced the task of taking the Merville battery and neutralising its guns. This force, down to to 150 men without heavy weapons, was about to enter into one of the most desperate struggles of the D-Day invasion.

The battery (Widerstandsnest 01) situated at Merville was armed with what the Allied intelligence services believed to be four 150 mm long-range guns housed in thick concrete casemates. It thus posed a direct threat to the British sector on Sword Beach. The calibre of these guns, however, proved to have been overestimated, for once the battery had been captured it was discovered that it was in fact equipped with 100 mm Skoda howitzers. These were dangerous enough, though, given their rate of fire (six rounds a minute) and their maximum range of nearly 10,000 metres, which put Sword Beach well within striking distance, and allowed the Merville battery to cover the coast from the mouth of the Orne all the way to Lion-sur-Mer.

Down to 150 men, the 9th Battalion nevertheless proceeded to attack.

During the spring of 1944 the RAF bombed this target repeatedly, laying waste to the surrounding area but leaving the battery intact. It was therefore imperative that this threat be neutralised by a direct assault before the invasion began. The job was given to the 9th Parachute Battalion, reinforced by men assigned from the 2nd Troop of the 591st Squadron, Royal Engineers. The German garrison was reckoned by the British to have between 180-200 men who had use of twenty machine guns and one four-barrelled anti-aircraft gun. The site of the battery was enclosed by two rings of barbed wire, an anti-tank ditch along the northwest flank, and minefields on the other three sides.

An aerial reconnaissance photo of the Merville battery. The number of bomb craters is noticeable, as is the anti-tank ditch along the northwest edge. (photo IWM)

The colour photo shows the site today.

Lieutenant Otway's men planned the operation to the last detail. They trained night and day on a life-size replica created in record time in the Berkshire countryside, near Newbury. The assault was laid out according to a bold plan timed to the minute. The 9th Parachute Battalion would arrive fifty minutes after midnight in Dropping Zone V, between Petitville and Varaville. This zone would have been marked out beforehand by two sticks from the 22nd Independent Parachute Company, slated to come in thirty minutes in advance. Two small advance parties from the 9th Battalion would arrive with these pathfinders; the first had orders to set up the rendezvous point where the assault troops would form up, while the second would reconnoitre the approaches to the battery and open lanes through the minefields. The heavy equipment, i.e. mortars, Bangalore torpedoes, small footbridges, mine detectors, and two 6-pounder anti-tank guns from the 4th Airlanding Anti-Tank Battery would come by glider to DZ V and and from there be transported by jeep. In the meantime, between midnight and 04h00, the Merville battery would receive its portion of the 5,268 tons of bombs which Bomber Command planned to unload on ten batteries along the Normandy coast. Even if these strikes missed the mark, they would presumably have a debilitating effect on the defenders.

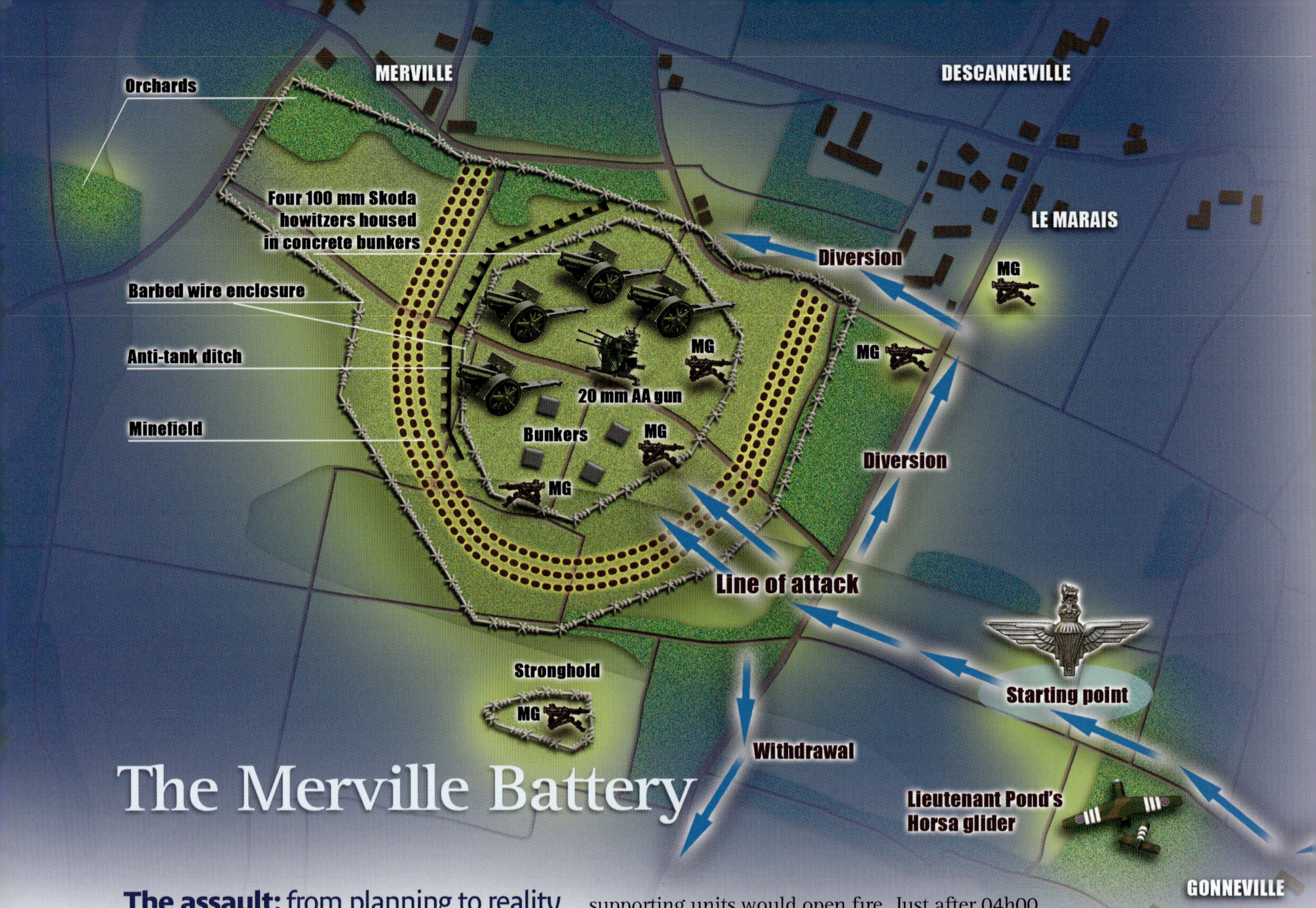

The Merville Battery

The assault: from planning to reality

After linking up with the advance parties, the troops setting out from DZ V were to proceed as follows:

- The assault force would move in from the southwest and follow three paths opened up in the enemy defences. These paths were to have been made by three advance platoons who would be followed immediately by the assault company using the first path.
- The reserve company would take the second path.
- Two sniping parties would take positions on each side of the battery, at a distance of about 140 metres. Each party would consist of three snipers, three men armed with Bren Guns, and three with anti-tank weapons.
- The two 6-pounder guns would be set up about 140 metres west of the battery.
- A diversionary force armed with five PIATs and two Bren Guns would cover the main approach on the northern side. This group would also have two German-speaking paratroopers.
- A base position under the officer second in command would be established 300 metres from the openings to the assault paths.
- The 3" mortars would be set up in a battery about 450 metres behind the base position.

Silence would reign as much as possible while gaps were cut in the barbed wire. In case of an alert, a bugle would sound "charge!" and the supporting units would open fire. Just after 04h00 three Horsa gliders would begin their descent onto the battery, guided by Eureka marking beacons. A minute later the bugle would sound "Reveille" and one of the mortars would fire a rocket flare to direct the gliders. At 04h28 the bugle would play "Assembly," at which point all would cease firing while the gliders landed. These would bring straight into the teeth of the enemy defences fifty paratroopers and eight sappers, armed with Sten Mark V machine pistols, grenades, and "General Wade" demolition charges. These men were to take care of the two guns in the centre of the battery; the assault teams moving in from the outside would spread out among the four casemates and eliminate the gunners while the sappers sabotaged the guns. If it did not receive a radio signal notifying it of the operation's success, the cruiser HMS Arethusa would open fire on the battery at 05h30.

Sad to say, this meticulously laid out plan would be upset by many cruel strokes of fortune. The first saw one of the three assault gliders snap its tow cable while still over England, although it managed to return its twenty-eight passengers safely to the ground. No. 67, headed for DZ V, had no such luck. It went down in the Channel with no survivors. Over the French coast, the Dakota aircrafts of the 47th Group encountered heavy fire which scattered their formations and resulted in a wide dispersal of the men dropped.

At the rendezvous point, the situation report was grim: only 150 men were on hand, instead of the intended 750, and not one of the gliders had arrived at DZ V. Hence no jeeps, no guns, no mine detectors, no crossing equipment, and no mortars. The only heavy weapon was a Vickers machine gun. There were enough radios, but just ten of the expected 120 Bangalore torpedoes. The two sniping parties were down to one at half strength; the medical personnel consisted of a single doctor and six orderlies; and all the sappers were missing. Otway nevertheless decided to go with what he had. Two teams of fifteen men would open paths for four groups which would attack the casemates. The Vickers gun would cover the left flank and a sergeant leading six paratroopers would make a diversion on the right. At 04h30, just as the assault began, the two surviving gliders flew over the zone searching in vain for the mortar rockets that were supposed to guide them. The "Tug" towing glider no. 27 made six passes over the battery before spotting a signal from the ground and releasing its companion. The glider came down in an orchard a hundred metres from Widersstandsnest 01. Bursting out at once, Lieutenant Hugh Pond and his men engaged a company of German infantry which had been preparing to attack Otway's troops. The "Tug" towing Horsa no. 28 made four turns before releasing it. Piloted by Staff-Sergeants Stanley Bone and L. Dean, came down 200 metres from the battery where a vicious struggle was going on. On the right flank Sergeant Sidney Knight silenced three machine gun posts with his Sten gun and grenades, an action for which he received the Military Medal. On the other side, the paratroopers manning the Vickers gun, Sergeant Pat McGeever and Corporal Jim McGuinness, also knocked out three enemy machine gun nests. Once the casemates were captured, the Skoda guns were put out of action by Gammon grenades. The damage seemed sufficient and the paratroopers evacuated the battery in case HMS Arethusa had not been notified and opened fire. Five officers and 65 paratroopers had been killed or wounded during the battle. Otway fell back on Le Hauger and Amfreville; in the first of these localities Lieutenant Thomas Halliburton was killed during an encounter with an enemy unit made up of Russian volunteers. It was a 9th Parachute Battalion barely a hundred men strong which took up defensive positions around the Chateau of Amfreville before being reinforced by No. 6 Commando in the early afternoon of June 6th.

June 6th, at l'Ecarde crossroads, Private Durston of 'A' Company, 9th Parachute Battalion, searches an enemy prisoner. Durston was one of the 64 members of his company supposed to arrive by glider at the battery. Note that he wears on his Denison Smock the skull and crossbones identifying the men in this group. (photo © IWM)

Evening of June 6th. At the command post of the 9th Battalion, Staff-Sergeant L. Dean (right) displays a captured Luger in the company of two Canadians, one a wounded paratrooper, the other a downed pilot. Dean co-piloted Horsa no. 28 which was supposed to land inside the battery enclosure. Over the breast pocket of his smock he wears the "Jolly Roger" identification worn by the men carried by all three gliders in the assault. (photo PAC)

This Mark II helmet riddled with bullet holes is a relic left by one of the units that fought alongside the 6th Airborne. It was found by a young inhabitant of Merville-Franceville.

Before finding the helmet above, the same young Norman picked up these leaflets at Merville-Franceville on June 6th.

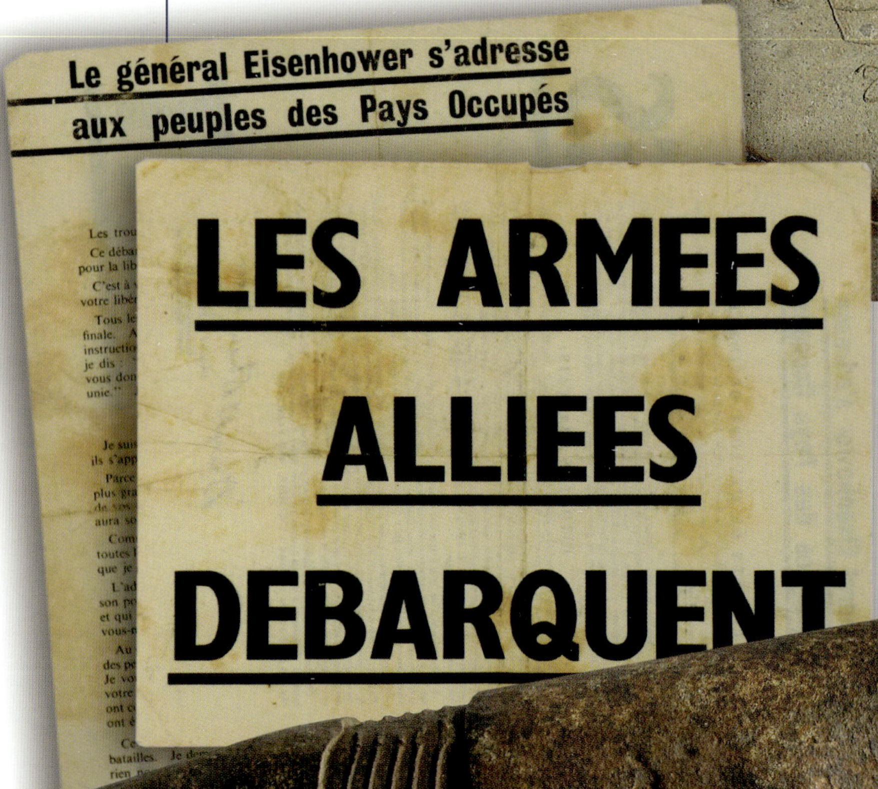

Le général Eisenhower s'adresse aux peuples des Pays Occupés

LES ARMEES ALLIEES DEBARQUENT

The Wehrmacht eagle and the date 26.7.1941 carved into the concrete of an anti-aircraft gun shelter at the Merville Battery.

A 150 mm naval shell, found in 2000 near Salenelles, probably fired by HMS Arethusa.

© Shell from the Pegasus Memorial; the other objects are in private collections.

The soldiers of Merville
Paratroopers and Commandos

A group from the 9th Parachute Battalion photographed before D-Day. Note the touch of humour supplied by the man standing on the right who is giving the photographer an enthusiastic "thumbs up." (photo Pegasus Memorial / DR)

The extraordinary assault by the paratroopers of the 9th Battalion on the night of June 5th-6th did not silence the Merville battery once and for all. As it turned out, a surviving German NCO was somehow able to get two guns firing again. Fortunately, the damage done to the guns limited their rate of fire to one round every ten minutes; still, shells did hit the landing beaches and the battery had to be attacked again in the afternoon of June 7th, this time by No. 3 Commando under Lieutenant-Colonel Peter Young.

Private Emile Corteil with his dog Glen. (photo Pegasus Memorial / DR)

Glen, the paratroop dog

Private Emile Servais Corteil, aged 19, was one of the dog-handlers of the 9th Battalion. On June 6th he jumped with his faithful companion Glen: both were killed that day. They lie at rest together in the Ranville War Cemetery. Besides Glen, other dogs served in the 3rd Battalion from January of 1943 on.

The idea originated with Brigadier Hill, and although they were used officially as messengers, Hill later confessed, *"they were really just a sideshow to keep the men amused."* Each of these Alsatians jumped with a specially adapted bicycle parachute and accompanied its designated master in combat.

Tom Holroyd's regulation cutlery inscribed with his army number.

Tom Holroyd at the end of the war.
(photo St-Martin / DR)

"Blimey Airborne" exclaims this exhausted paratrooper. Humour helped men bear up under the intensive training done by airborne troops which the drawing reflects. Still, the pride of belonging to an elite unit comes through just as strongly.

A paratrooper's small good luck charm. Attached to the ring of a grenade are bits of parachute cord, each one marking a successful jump.

An "economy issue" plastic cap badge of the Parachute Regiment.

Escape map of synthetic silk given to Tom Holroyd and his fellow paratroopers; they were also given out among the glider pilots and commandos. They could be concealed in various ways and were often sewn into the lining of the soldier's blouse.

From the pockets of a D-Day paratrooper

All the objects shown on this page were taken along for the invasion by Tom Holroyd, of 'C' Company in the 12th Parachute Battalion. They included a humorous drawing in his own hand showing him, overloaded and utterly worn out, cursing the airborne service after a route march of forty-five miles. Visible beside his signature is the motto of the 6th Airborne Division, "Go to it."

A saw to be used in an escape, also to be hidden in the uniform.

Shaving brush marked with Holroyd's army number. A "Tommy" on campaign shaved every day.

Tube of morphine to relieve pain at once if wounded.

This remarkable model of the railway bridge at Bures was made in Britain and used to prepare the sappers of the 3rd Parachute Squadron for their demolition operation.

The destruction of the bridges
over the Dives River at Troarn and Bures

To prevent the Germans from launching a counterattack against the British bridgehead from the east side of the Orne, the bridges over the Dives had to be blown. Lieutenant-Colonel Alastair Pearson's 8th Parachute Battalion had to capture Troarn and cover the sappers of the 3rd Parachute Squadron, Royal Engineers, while they destroyed the bridge as well as the two structures at Bures, two kilometres to the north.

The 8th Parachute Battalion also suffered a wide dispersion during the drop and a good many of its men ended up in DZ N instead of DZ K. What happened was that shortly after midnight several pathfinders heading for DZ K had in fact come to DZ N and in good faith sent the wrong signal. On top of that, when he got to the rendezvous point at the Touffreville crossroads at 01h20, Lieutenant-Colonel Pearson was appalled to find only an RE jeep with its trailer and thirty paratroopers. A few minutes later a prisoner revealed that Troarn was defended by two hundred men with half-tracks. At 03h30, after rallying a number of scattered men, Pearson had at his disposal a motley force consisting of four paratroopers from 'A' Company, two officers and twenty-seven other ranks, plus a Bren Gun, from 'B' Company, and three officers and seventy-two men from 'C' company. Battalion headquarters had two PIATs and counted six officers and thirty men from different services, among them medical orderlies, signallers, and eight glider pilots. The six men from the Royal Engineers had two jeeps with trailers, while the signallers carried two types of radio which in normal circumstances allowed communication with brigade headquarters. It seemed a tall order to try to take Troarn with these 150 men; moreover, the explosives that they had on hand would not be powerful enough to bring down the sturdy stone bridge standing on five arches. On the other hand, they could do serious damage to the smaller bridges at Bures supported by lattice girders. Pearson deemed it best to wait until he had assembled a force large enough to be able to attack Troarn. In anticipation of this action, he despatched a sizeable patrol to explore the outskirts of the town, placed his PIATs between Touffreville and Le Mesnil, and concealed his troops in the woods near Bures.

A handful of sappers from the 3rd Para Squadron destroyed the bridges over the Dives River.

At the same time the larger part of Major Tim Roseveare's 3rd Parachute Squadron, Royal Engineers, had landed in DZ N. The major had realised to his surprise that the Drop Zone was crawling with paratroopers from all units of the 6th Airborne. He gathered his own men and equipment and carried out an emergency reorganisation. All in all, the sappers had more than two tons' worth of explosives but only six collapsible trolleys by way of transport... nevertheless, these would carry enough to wreck the bridges at Troarn and Bures. Sixty of Roseveare's men accompanied by about thirty paratroopers of the 8th Battalion (who had lost contact with their own officers) set off in the direction of the bridges over the Dives. On the way they were joined by a jeep and trailer from the Royal Army Medical Corps. A little while later they came across two officers from the 8th Battalion, whereupon Major Roseveare returned the men from their unit to them and ordered them to hold on to the crossroads west of Troarn.

The bridge over the Dives on the way out of Troarn as it is today. The inset photo shows the plaque commemorating the actions of Major Roseveare and his men on the night of June 5th-6th, 1944.

Destruction of **the Dives bridges**

The sappers then divided into two groups. The first group, the major and eight men, would use the medical jeep and its trailer to go to Troarn and blow up the bridge; for this task they would take all the "General Wade" charges available. The second group included the rest of the sappers under the command of Captain Thomas "Tim" Juckes. He set off in the direction of Bures with all the plastic explosive stacked on the trolleys. After a stealthy passage through Bois de Bures, Juckes's group arrived at the bridges at 06h30 without meeting opposition. The sappers immediately got to work. They were joined by men from the 8th Battalion coming from Drop Zone K. Lieutenant-Colonel Pearson had lent them one of the jeeps with a trailer which helped to transport the explosives. Lieutenant Alan Wade then took the jeep to try to have a look at the bridge at Troarn but was dissuaded from doing so by French civilians who reported the hue and cry raised by the enemy. Wade then opted for a less obvious approach and made his way on foot towards Troarn and the bridge. En route he came across a bogged down jeep and found the bridge had been destroyed. Back he went to Bures to report his findings. There the charges had been set on the two bridges, and at 09h30 both went tumbling into the Dives, broken in half. To revive his exhausted men, Captain Juckes gave them time to have a most welcome breakfast before vacating the premises. Meanwhile, a few hours earlier Major Roseveare's little band had made its way through the woods towards Troarn. Despite their watchful advance the jeep became ensnarled in a tangle of barbed wire that was part of a road barrier. A German guard let fly a burst before vanishing, but it took nearly twenty minutes to free the jeep with the aid of wire-cutters. The team started off again, forgetting Sapper Moon who was left behind... At the crossroads before Troarn, two paratroopers sent ahead on foot as scouts attempted to take a German cyclist prisoner, but when he put up a fight one of the paratroopers made the mistake of shooting him with his Sten gun. That set off the alarm in Troarn and flares soon lit up the sky. Everyone bundled into the jeep which raced off into the village in a bid to reach the bridge on the far side. Despite Major Roseveare's best efforts, the ride was nothing but a mad rush in slow motion – pulling a trailer loaded with explosives and burdened further with eight fully equipped paratroopers, a combined weight calculated by Roseveare at 1,360 kilograms (i.e. one and a half tons), the poor vehicle could go no faster than 55 kilometres an hour. Once it hit the main road

The bridge at Troarn before its destruction.

Model of the bridge at Troarn used to instruct British sappers in preparation for their operations on D-Day.

The plaque by the bridge at Troarn today.

Major Tim Roseveare, DSO, photographed in Germany, not far from Wismar, in May 1945. (photo Pegasus Memorial / DR)

This German map was marked up on June 7th, 1944 and notes the destruction of the bridges at Troarn and Bures. (doc NARA).

which led straight down to the bridge, all hell broke loose. In Roseveare's own words, *"At the corner the fun started. There seemed to be a Boche in every doorway shooting like mad. However, the boys got to work with their Sten guns and Sapper Peachey did very good work as rear gunner with the Bren gun."* Peachey in fact worked his gun while perched on the explosives in the trailer but by some miracle no bullets hit this volatile cargo. The steep slope in the road allowed the jeep to pick up speed even as it wobbled precariously because of the trailer's weight. Jeep, trailer, and cargo finally made it through the village, its passengers escorted by tracer bursts from an MG 34 that passed just over their heads. Once arrived at the bridge Roseveare noticed Peachey's absence. The Bren gunner had been wounded, fallen off the trailer, and been taken prisoner. As the bridge was unguarded, the sappers quickly set 49 "General Wade" charges under the central arch. The explosion ripped open a wide breach in the structure. The group then tried to reach Bures by driving along the bank of the Dives but the jeep got stuck and had to be left in the spot where Lieutenant Wade found it several hours later. Since Bures was assumed to be in enemy hands, Roseveare and his men headed for Le Mesnil which they reached around 13h00. At mid-day Lieutenant-Colonel Pearson, who had not yet received confirmed reports of the destruction of the Troarn bridge, sent a detachment to carry out or finish the job. This little caravan included a handful of sappers under the command of Captain Juckes who had a jeep loaded with 40 "General Wade" charges at his disposal; a platoon from the 8th Battalion, commanded by Lieutenant Colin Brown, was ordered to go along with them. The paratroopers kept the Germans busy in the village so as to allow the sappers to reach the bridge. They got there after a few brushes with the enemy, and at 15h00 a new explosion widened the existing breach to 10-12 metres. The group made it back to Pearson's command post an hour and a half later, while for their part Brown's men brought back seven prisoners from the 21st Panzer Division.

Despite the difficulties caused by their far-flung dispersion, the 8th Parachute Battalion and the 3rd Parachute Squadron had carried out their assignments. Major Roseveare received the DSO for his actions, Captain Juckes (sadly, to die three weeks later from a mortar blast) the Military Cross.

The tools of the paratroop sappers

It was on this kind of "Collapsible Trolley" that Captain Juckes's men transported the explosives used to blow up the bridges at Bures.

© The objects shown on these pages come from the collections of the Pegasus Memorial in Ranville.

Major Roseveare's group opened the first breach in the Troarn bridge with forty-nine of these "General Wade" charges.

Tube containing ten primers Guncotton Mark III.

Pliers to set the detonators.

A "box of crayons" holding delay fuses.

Detail of a Royal Engineers officer's bullion insignia.

Beret of an Royal Engineers officer serving with the Airborne troops.

The vehicles
of the 3rd Parachute Squadron

These pages illustrate the two means of transport used by Roseveare and Juckes on their missions. The jeep was the basic vehicle in the airborne divisions, which had 904 each. The "Collapsible trolley," a sturdy folding cart, could carry materiel in the absence of vehicular transport. It was used like a wheelbarrow, but several men could put their weight behind it to push it along when fully loaded.

This typical airborne jeep gives some idea of the one used by Major Roseveare in his raid on the bridge at Troarn. The jeeps transported by glider underwent several basic modifications: the bumper was shorted at the ends, the grab handles, rear-view mirror, and the tool carrier were all taken off.

Battle dress blouse worn by Private Thomas Hendry of the 225th Parachute Field Ambulance.

The markings on this folding stretcher show that it belonged to the 195th Airlanding Field Ambulance.

Photo and the Hospital Redirection Card of Private Tom Thresher, 13th Para Battalion wounded on August 19th, 1944.

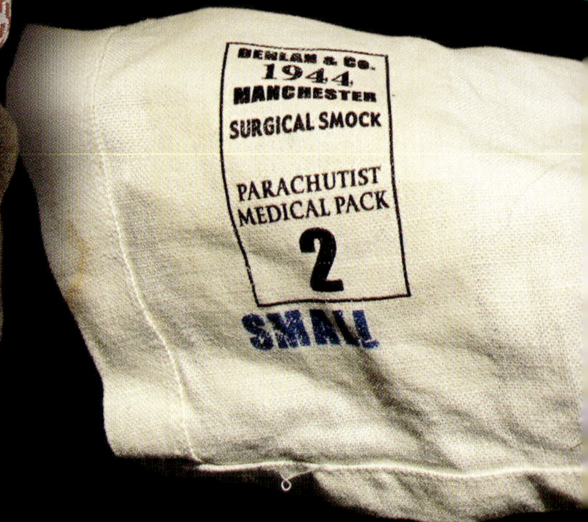

Surgical smock specially adapted for use by the Airborne's medical personnel.

Evacuation labels to be attached to the wounded.

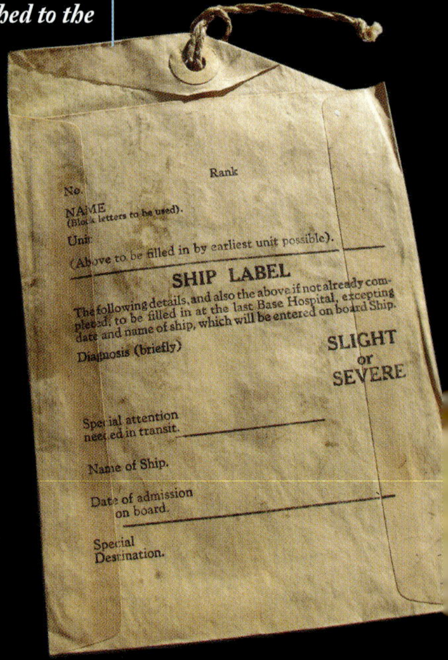

This impressive collection of decorations won in two world wars belonged to Lieutenant-Colonel Malcolm MacEwan who commanded the medical services of the 6th Airborne Division — it earned him the affectionate nickname, "Old Technicolour."

Private Bertram H. Roe was a conscientious objector who nevertheless served in the Royal Army Medical Corps. He volunteered for the airborne forces in 1943 and was assigned to the 225th Parachute Field Ambulance. He jumped with the 13th Battalion on June 6th; five weeks later, on July 10th, during a three-hour enemy bombardment, he tended to and evacuated the wounded, even going so far as to shield one of them with his own body. For this courageous act he received the Military Medal.

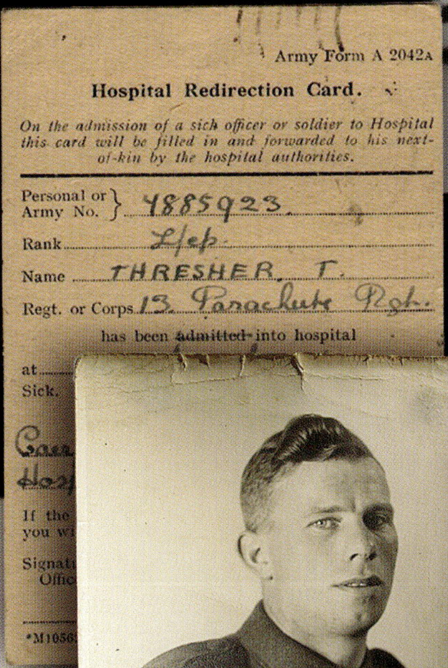
Army Form A 2042A

Hospital Redirection Card.

On the admission of a sick officer or soldier to Hospital this card will be filled in and forwarded to his next-of-kin by the hospital authorities.

Personal or Army No. 4885923
Rank L/Cpl.
Name THRESHER T.
Regt. or Corps 13. Parachute Rgt.
has been ~~admitted~~ into hospital
at
Sick.

The paratroopers who wore a Red Cross

Royal Army Medical Corps

Part of the first wave, the medical personnel came by glider or by parachute. Doctors, ambulance drivers, and specialised orderlies accompanied the fighting men and shared their risks. More than one hundred of these medics had indicated their wish not to take up arms; they were conscientious objectors who volunteered to serve their country and their comrades.

A drawing taken from a humorous fresco done by Private Thomas Hendry while serving in Normandy with the 225th Parachute Field Ambulance. It depicts the daily experience of the medical orderly in a style parodying the Bayeux Tapestry.

CANADIAN PARACHUTE CORPS

Canadian parachute qualification badge.

The 1st Canadian Parachute Battalion at Varaville and Robehomme

Parachuted into Drop Zone V fifty minutes after midnight on June 6th, the companies of the Canadian battalion had to go their separate ways to carry out their assignments. 'A' Company would protect the 9th Parachute Battalion's left flank during its attack on the Merville battery. 'B' Company was ordered to destroy the bridge at Robehomme, 'C' Company the one at Varaville, as well as any enemy positions in the vicinity.

Faces of 'C' Company. Above, left to right: Corporal Dan Hartigan and Lieutenant Samuel McGowan (killed in Germany on March 28th, 1945); below, left to right, Private William Chaddock (died of wounds on June 20th, 1944) and Private Andrew McNally (killed in Germany on March 24th, 1945). (photos PAC)

Beneath the photographs is the cap badge of the 1st Canadian Parachute Battalion.

On June 5th at 22h00, 'C' Company boarded Albemarle bombers; the company was to be dropped at the same time as the pathfinders of the 22nd Independent Company in order to eliminate all enemy presence from Drop Zone V. It would then proceed to Varaville with sappers of the 3rd Parachute Squadron, Royal Engineers, there to destroy the bridge over the Divette. While in this area the unit was also to neutralise an enemy communications centre, a strongpoint featuring a 75 mm gun, and more generally to deal with any enemy garrison it came across. The rest of the Canadian battalion, to be transported by Dakotas, took off from Down Ampney at 23h00. Like their British comrades in arms, the Canadians were met by intense anti-aircraft fire, and like their counterparts they would as a result be badly dispersed. A good many men from 'C' Company came to earth west of the Dives, nowhere near DZ V which was located west of the Divette. Lieutenant John Madden's stick of paratroopers found themselves on the west bank of the Orne River, of all places, just a kilometre or so from the landing beaches.

'C' Company was therefore not of much use to the pathfinders ordered to set up the Drop Zone. At the company's rendezvous point, Major Hugh Murray MacLeod could find only eight paratroopers. They made their way together towards the chateau of Varaville, one of their objectives that night. Other strays from 'C' Company were also heading in that direction, so that Major MacLeod saw his meagre forces strengthened by a group led by Lieutenant "Chug" Walker and another led by Private Fred Rudko. In the meantime the aerial bombardment of the Merville battery was underway and a few misaimed bombs landed not far from the Canadians who, even if they came out of it alive, were badly shocked. MacLeod's men nonetheless reached Varaville where they chanced upon a number of sappers from the 3rd Parachute Squadron. They were the beneficiaries of no less a haphazard drop than the one the Canadians had made. That they even got to the place where they were to carry out their assignment testifies to their tenacity and professionalism. Dropped into the flooded areas east of Varaville, the sappers had succeeded in retrieving many of their explosives containers from the water. Lieutenant Jack Inman and twelves sappers transported three of these across swampy ground and ditches as far as Varaville where they found one of their missing officers, Lieutenant Pat Baillie. Inman left five sappers and ninety kilos of explosives with him before striking out for the bridge at Robehomme. Covered by a few Canadian paratroopers, Baillie's group placed their explosives. At 04h40

Normandy was the first theatre of operations for the Canadian Red Devils.

the charges were set off and a four-metre gap was left in the bridge over the Divette.

During this time the party led by Major MacLeod and Lieutenant Hugh Walker carried on with their assignment at the Varaville chateau. Beside the chateau, at a crossroads, the Germans had created a strongpoint armed with machine guns, mortars, and a 75 mm gun. MacLeod and his men reached the guardhouse at the entrance to the estate without being seen. This large building obviously served as a barracks but the paratroopers found it unoccupied. MacLeod and Walker deployed their men around the building and went up to the second floor to observe the German positions, which consisted of a long trench reinforced by pillboxes and a bunker at either end. The Germans opened up with machine guns and mortars and even the 75 mm gun added its contribution to the fire directed at the building. To silence this weapon, MacLeod had Corporal Winslow Oikle come up with his PIAT. His first attempt fell short and the 75's riposte scored a direct hit on the PIAT's ammunition. The explosion killed Corporal Oikle outright, as well as Lieutenant Walker, Private John Jowett, and Private Leslie Neufeld. Major MacLeod and his runner Private Peter Bismutka died of their wounds shortly afterwards. The paratroopers at Varaville were now led by Captain John Hanson, second in command of 'C' Company, who arrived moments later. Other groups dispersed in the landings showed up little by little. Lieutenant Sam McGowan's group reached the village just in time to take out two German detachments arriving as reinforcements. At the chateau, two stray paratroopers, Corporal Dan Hartigan and Private W.C. Mallon, arrived with a 2" mortar; a few hours earlier, Hartigan had landed in an apple tree, 450 metres from his drop zone.

At 08h30, after a stand-off of several hours between the paratroopers and defenders, the sound of the bridge blowing up heartened the former and took the fight out of the latter. Around mid-morning Hartigan brought his mortar up to the enemy positions by crawling through a ditch; from close range he fired four bombs in quick succession, then used several smoke shells to screen his withdrawal. Every shot hit the target and the forty-three surviving Germans surrendered, putting an end to the battle at Varaville. 'C' Company held its position until evening when it was relieved by Commandos of the 1st Special Service Brigade. Captain Hanson and his men rejoined the rest of the battalion at Le Mesnil. 'A' Company had been so affected by the dispersion that only Lieutenant Jack Clancy and two or three other

Opposite page: above, left, Major Hugh McLeod, aged 25, commander of 'C' Company, killed at Varaville on June 6th. (photo DR)

Below, left, Private Marcel Lanthier, aged 21, an American volunteer of French-Canadian descent, killed on June 9th. On right, armed with a Colt .45, Company Sergeant Major W.I. Blair of 'B' Company. (photos PAC)

men turned up at the rendezvous point. After doing some reconnaissance around Gonneville-en-Auge, Clancy returned to the rendezvous point at 06h00 and collected about twenty paratroopers from various units. These men he took to provide cover for the 9th Battalion's withdrawal, his little group protecting the rear of Otway's unit as far as Le Plein. Clancy and his men then set off for Le Mesnil which they reached in mid-afternoon. 'B' Company was in large part scattered over flooded swamps, which resulted in the complete or partial loss of their equipment for many paratroopers. Several unfortunate ones drowned, enmeshed in their harnesses or parachute cords. Lieutenant Norm Toseland was lucky enough to come down on dry land but could find only one fellow paratrooper, Sergeant Joe LaCasse, with whom he headed off for the bridge at Robehomme. As they hurried along they fell in with a dozen men from 'B' Company and a few British paratroopers from the 8th and 9th Battalions. Skilfully guided through a swamp by a young French woman, they came to the Robehomme bridge at 03h00. There he found Major Clayton Fuller who had landed not far from the spot – right in the middle of the Dives River. The few sappers from the 3rd Parachute Squadron were unfortunately without much of their detonating equipment; but Sergeant Bill Poole came up with the notion of concocting some sort of giant "Gammon" grenade out of all the individual plastic charges the paratroopers had. The 13 kilos or so of explosives cobbled together succeeded only in damaging the structure. Midway through the morning, Lieutenant Jack Inman and his sappers finally arrived in Robehomme after trekking on foot from Varaville. Since the flooded ground had made it impossible to use the collapsible trolleys, his men had carried ninety kilos of explosives on their backs across the swampy landscape. The persevering officer then set his charges, and at 11h00 the explosions made two enormous breaches in the bridge. As they were placing the explosives, however, the sappers had come under fire from enemy soldiers arriving in trucks. The paratroopers managed to hold off the Germans while the sappers did their work, and then all fell back upon the village under covering fire from a Bren gun. Canadians and British took up positions along the high ground at Robehomme, then rejoined 1st Canadian Parachute Battalion during the night of June 7th-8th.

Signal Platoon 9th Parachute Battalion

This uniform belong to Signaller William Stack. The red shoulder tabs identify him as a member of the 9th Parachute Battalion. With the exception of the 12th Devonshire, each regiment of the three brigades wore shoulder tabs with distinct colours identifying it.

William Stack's red beret.

Stack's specialised role of Qualified Signaller was indicated by the insignia sewn onto the lower left sleeve.

On the upper right sleeve, the "Pegasus" emblem of the airborne troops, surmounted by a paratrooper's brevet and the shoulder flash of the Parachute Regiment.

The Signals Platoon of the 9th Parachute Battalion in 1944.
(photo Pegasus Memorial / DR)

William Stack, in the centre of the photograph.

« ...That whosoever believeth in Him should not perish... »

In 1941, 17-year old Fred Milward left home to enlist in the army. Two women from his village presented him with a New Testament which they had marked on the inside cover with "St. John III. 16." Having become a signaller with the 9th Parachute Battalion, Milward took his New Testament with him to Normandy. During the intense fighting around the chateau at St-Côme the young soldier found comfort in reading the verse noted.
He kept his scriptural vademecum with him for many years. It was stained with the blood of his friend Sidney Harmer, wounded in the Bois-de-Bavent.

The New Testament given to Millward. The page with the verse marked by the two ladies who presented it to him remains folded.

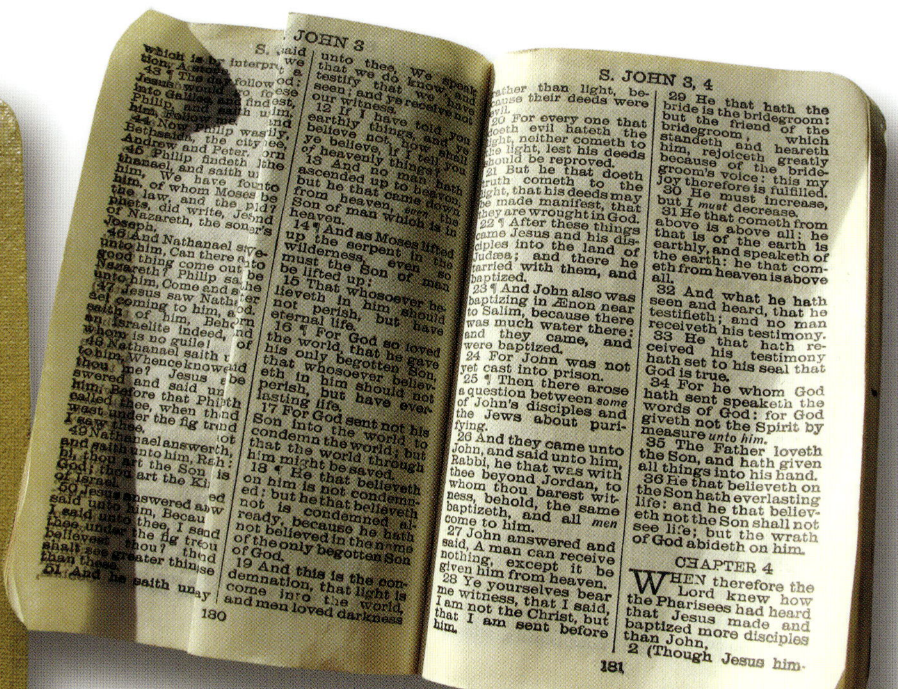

Lieutenants and brothers: Joseph Philippe Rousseau (left), who died on June 6th, 1944, and Joseph Maurice Rousseau, who was killed fighting with the SAS in Alsace on September 20, 1944. They rest side by side in the Ranville War Cemetery, two proud French Canadians who "fell on the earth from which their forefathers came." (photo PAC)

Far from the Drop Zones, the "castaways" of the 6th Airborne Division

Dropped in desperation by aircraft in distress or trapped on board gliders that had lost their way, a great many British and Canadians of the 6th Airborne Division would come to earth far from the intended Drop Zones or Landing Zones. A number made it back to the divisional sector after days of wandering through unknown country, but others never stood a chance.

The tragic odyssey of Lieutenant Rousseau's group

During the night of June 5th-6th, at the end of a very disrupted flight, Dakota transport KG 367 dropped its passengers in chaotic circumstances. The men were scattered to the winds and it took hours for them to come together in little clusters. Twenty in all, they belonged to No. 4 Platoon, 'B' Company, of the 1st Canadian Parachute Battalion. Their leader was Lieutenant Philippe Rousseau of Montreal. They had been heading for Drop Zone V near Varaville, but found themselves dispersed about a dozen kilometres to the northeast, between Gonneville-sur-Mer and Douville. Lieutenant Rousseau found five of his men, Privates Broadfoot, Oxtoby, Pastorius, Moffat, and McKenzie. When morning came, the little group was by the brickworks in Gonneville-sur-Mer where it came under fire from a German machine gun. Rousseau and Oxtoby were killed instantly – a bullet caused one of the phosphorous grenades carried by the lieutenant to explode so that his body was partly burned. McKenzie, wounded, was captured. Moffat and Broadfoot managed to get away, but the first would later be captured, while the second would be killed the next day after rejoining his comrades from No. 4 Platoon. Pastorius was taken prisoner and spent the rest of the war in captivity, returning home to enter university and embark on a long medical career.

During the ride on the Dakota, another ill-fated paratrooper, Private Alex "Snuffy" MacInnis had announced to his comrades, "Boys, I have the feeling that I won't be coming back." He was reported missing on June 6th, and his body was never found. Sergeant D.N. Beaudoin who had also succeeded in collecting a few paratroopers was wounded and captured on the railway line at Gonneville. Private Stan Shulist, whose legs were badly injured on landing, was captured early in the morning. He had to have a leg amputated at Deauville. Wounded at the same time as Beaudoin, Sergeant I.H. Trenholm was also taken prisoner.

On June 7th, eleven survivors from Dakota KG 367 formed a provisional unit with fifteen British paratroopers, among whom were several medical personnel, all of them conscientious objectors who were accordingly unarmed.

Worn out from hours on the move and the tension, the paratroopers decided to take up a position in a pasture bordered by a hedgerow and wait for nightfall before resuming their march. The Canadians there were Corporal G.A. McWilliams, Lance Corporal B.M. Anderson, as well as paratroopers G.C. Connaghan, K.M. Pledger, J.G. Broadfoot, B.M. Isley, G.R. Robertson, A.A. Schillemore, J. MacPherson, T.O. Willsey, and M.O. Ellefson. Unfortunately they had been spotted and encircled by a much larger force equipped with mortars. A fight as confusing as it was violent then broke out. In front of several witnesses Private Connaghan brought down a tall German soldier before he himself crumpled face down to the ground. Boyd Anderson, who survived the battle, described many years after the war the horror of that day and the sight of his friends being killed in just a few seconds: "Just about this time more fire came down the line. Broadfoot's brains were blown out his helmet. Pledger collapsed over his rifle. Ellefson shook with a few muscular tremors and turned over on his back, dead ... Pledger and Broadfoot were just kids out of Toronto. Ellefson, a more mature fellow, was from Saskatoon. Ellefson and I had been in the same platoon and section for two years. We had never had a cross word, his money was my money, mine was his." Alongside the four Canadians a half dozen British were killed in the engagement. Robertson and Schillemore, both wounded, were taken prisoner, as were their comrades McWilliams, Isley, and Willsey. MacPherson and Lance Corporal Anderson, who was wounded, got to a barn where they barely evaded the Germans by hiding in a large cider barrel. At the end of three days, followed by a week's wandering hither and thither, the two Canadians met a French couple who guided them to a group of Allied soldiers made up of British paratroopers and airmen who had been shot down. On June 16th, Anderson was captured along with several of his companions in misfortune. MacPherson managed to reach the American lines after the closing of the Falaise pocket – the only member of Lieutenant Rousseau's group to come out of Normandy free and alive, he rejoined the 1st Canadian Parachute Battalion and fought in Belgium, Holland, and Germany.

June 5th, the day before the invasion. Lieutenant Philippe Rousseau, on the left, stands beside fellow lieutenants Toseland and Harrison. (photo PAC)

The gas mask that belonged to Private A. Schillemore, and one of his identity discs. It was found close to the place where he was taken prisoner.

© The objects shown on these pages come from the collections of the Pegasus Memorial in Ranville.

St-Vaast-en-Auge and Grangues

A long way from the drop zones, St-Vaast-en-Auge is nestled in the heart of rolling countryside unsuited to glider landings. Nevertheless, the hazards of war would bring several bands of red berets into its midst. Twelve of them would meet their death there. Just after midnight on June 6th, a Dakota hit by anti-aircraft fire went off course over the Auge region, one of its motors on fire. The eighteen passengers from the 1st Canadian Parachute Battalion made an emergency evacuation from the stricken aircraft. The paratroopers scattered into the night far from their drop zone. Once on the ground, three NCOs, Company Sergeant-Major L.B. Hall, Sergeant George LaCroix, and Sergeant Douglas Brown managed to regroup.

While they were carefully scouring the area in search of other men from the Dakota, the Canadians saw a Hamilcar glider come to earth in a nearby orchard. It was Hamilcar no. 501, nicknamed "The Bag of Bagdad," piloted by Staff-Sergeant L. Ridings and Sergeant R.A. Harris, and one of four Hamilcars used in Operation Tonga. Only two made it to their destination – no. 502 had been forced to land in England when its tow cable snapped in flight. The four heavy gliders had been loaded in the same way, with an invaluable 17-pounder anti-tank gun, its crew, and Morris C8 tractor intended for the drop zone at Ranville. It was likewise a snapped tow cable which brought "The Bag of Bagdad" to St-Vaast-en-Auge. After landing around 03h30, the two pilots and eight gunners from the 3rd Airlanding Anti-Tank Battery were joined by the three paratroop Canadians, Hall, LaCroix, and Brown. As highest ranking NCO, CSM Hall took charge of the group. To get some idea of where they were, they ventured into a local farm, the "Lieu Panier," where Hall and Brown asked directions from the farmers while the rest of the men waited about a hundred metres away behind a hedgerow. Alas, while the two NCOs were speaking with the Norman couple, gunshots rang out near the hedgerow. It appeared that the small group had been spotted by a German patrol. The balance sheet made grim reading: Bombardier William Whitney, Gunners Douglas Stanley and Frank Newham were killed. The Canadian sergeant, George LaCroix, was hit in the head and died shortly afterwards. Sergeant Leslie Ridings was badly wounded and lingered until the following day. In keeping with the orders to get glider pilots back quickly, the survivors decided to evacuate "The Bag of Bagdad's" other pilot, Sergeant Ronald Harris, who went off with the Canadians Hall and Brown. The five gunners from the 3rd Airlanding Anti-Tank Battery, Sergeant W. Cannon, Bombardier K. Harding, Gunner J. Grainger, et two others whose names are not known, offered to cover their departure. After holding on until the afternoon of June 6th, all were taken prisoner around 16h00. Four days later, Hall, Brown, and Harris, utterly exhausted, were captured near Pont-l'Evêque.

The helmet of Sergeant LaCroix, killed at St-Vaast-en-Auge.

June 3rd, 1944. Signalmen Easby (left) and Davis. Davis would died in the Horsa that crashed at St-Vaast. Easby, a dispatch rider, would go all the way through Normandy, the Ardennes, and Germany.

St-Vaast-en-Auge was the scene of another drama during the first hours of the invasion. At 02h45 a crippled Horsa, no. 35, heading for Ranville, crashed in the woods of the manor's farm. It had been under the controls of Staff-Sergeant C. Hopgood and Sergeant D. Phillips; on board were Captain S. Daisley, Quartermaster of the 13th Parachute Battalion, his batman Private J. Aldred, Signalman D. Davis, et two other soldiers whose names are not known. The Horsa was also carrying Captain Daisley's jeep and trailer and Signalman Davis's motorcycle. Hopgood, Phillips, Daisley, Aldred, and Davis were killed in the crash. The two survivors managed to hide the motorcycle beneath a railway trestle before they were taken prisoner two days later.

Grangues, too, saw a number of red berets descend upon its soil. Two Stirling bombers crashed not far from the chateau. The first was carrying twenty-five paratroopers of the 7th Battalion, none of whom survived. The second was to drop seventeen sappers from the 591st Parachute Squadron at Ranville. When it caught fire from anti-aircraft bursts, four paratroopers managed to bale out, but the others were blocked by the flames in the fuselage. One of them was Lieutenant John Shinner, Intelligence Officer at the Royal Engineers' headquarters. He described these terrible few minutes in his diary: *"The sky seemed to be full of vivid flashes and orange streaks. Suddenly there was a flash and a burst of flame inside the aircraft, astern of where I stood. In a matter of seconds the whole of the inside of the aircraft was blazing. Each of the sappers had been carrying 5lb sausages* of plastic explosive and one poor chap had his hit, and it burned fiercely. Five or six of us at the forward end of the fire were forced forward towards the main spar by the flames. I felt the flames singeing my face and yelled to someone to get the escape hatch off to let out the suffocating smoke. I told one of the sappers to go forward to the radio cabin to find out what the situation was. He contacted one of the crew, but obviously things were badly wrong up there, because they passed the order to jump and then immediately cancelled it. In any case we could not have got past the blaze between us and the exit hole."*

Three of the four men who jumped were captured, the fourth succeeding in rejoining the rest of his unit. The other Stirling made a crash landing not far from the first airplane. Two of its six-member crew and nine paratroopers survived the impact. They were all taken prisoner by soldiers from the German 711th Infantry Division who were occupying the chateau. Shortly afterwards, Horsa no. 90, piloted by Staff-Sergeant Roy Luff and Lieutenant John Bromley, crashed in the nearby woods. It had been transporting the Forward Observation Officers of the 5th Parachute Brigade and their radios. No one got out alive. Glider no. 74 fell behind the chateau, among the trees. The pilot, Staff-Sergeant Duncan Wright, died in the crash, as did two of his passengers. The co-pilot, Sergeant Barry Powell, was held captive in a stable along with the sappers who survived the Stirling's crash. During the morning these eight men were executed by the Germans on the pretext that they had attempted to escape. On the other hand, the survivors from a glider that crashed a little further away, were taken care of by the Germans in Pont-l'Evêque after they had been captured. A last Horsa seems to have succeeded in landing in this area without serious damage. All in all, fifty-two pilots and paratroopers lost their lives at Grangues.

** These "sausages" consisted of sticks of gelegnite slipped into the inner tube of a bicycle wheel. They were meant to blow up the tall wooden stakes ("Rommel's asparagus") planted in the ground as obstacles against glider landings.*

This German map, marked up on June 6th, shows the location of the groups of paratroopers dispersed and isolated, and indicates their "annihilation" (Vernichtet). To be noted is the sending of reinforcements from the 711th Division from Trouville.
(document NARA)

Prototype of the monument commemorating the link-up of the commandos and paratroopers at Bénouville. Both the model and the plaque of the monument were created by Maurice Chauvet, one of the 177 French commandos

Brigadier Lord Lovat, 24th Chief of the Clan Fraser and the commander of the 1st Special Service Brigade. (photo © IWM)

The Commandos of the 1st Special Service Brigade

This brigade came ashore on Sword Beach between 07h30 and 08h40. Its task was to eliminate the coastal battery at Ouistreham, then move quickly to the bridges at Bénouville and Ranville to reinforce the 6th Airborne Division already there. The brigade was led by the legendary Lord Lovat, one of the founding members of the Commandos. Lovat and his men reached Bénouville at 12h30 to the sound of bagpipes and proudly sporting their green berets. Panache aside, the bagpipes and berets had been noted in the instructions to the airborne soldiers as the identifying features of the commandos. The 1st and 4th Special Service Brigades would go through the entire campaign at the side of the 6th Airborne Division.

Shoulder title worn by Sergeant Jack Needler of the Intelligence Section of No. 6 Commando. (Private collection)

Fairbairn-Sykes fighting knife (3rd model), a dagger used by British special troops. The one shown here belonged to Piper Bill Millin.

Piper Bill Millin

In 1944, 21 year-old Bill Millin was serving in the demonstration team at the commando training centre at Achnacarry in the Scottish highlands. He was also one of the members of the camp's Pipe Band. He caught Lord Lovat's eye there and was appointed his personal piper in preparation for the invasion. On D-Day he played the 1st Special Service Brigade ashore on Sword Beach and on the march to Bénouville, thus earning a place in history.

Piper Millin plays for his comrades before embarkation. (photo © IWM)

Bill Millin coming ashore with his bagpipes on June 6th. (photo © IWM). *Below: the instrument is now on display at the Pegasus Memorial.*

© The objects shown on these pages come from the collections of the Pegasus Memorial in Ranville.

The chateau St-Côme, scene of fierce fighting by the 9th Battalion. (photo Pegasus Memorial /DR)

The bridgehead east of the Orne

June 7th - August 16th, 1944

On the morning of June 7th the 6th Airborne was still spread over a wide area. The enemy pressure was mounting and the Airborne had to reassemble its men and consolidate its positions east of the Orne River. For two and a half months, the red berets of the Airborne Division and the green berets of the Commandos would hold this strategically vital zone in order to protect the eastern flank of the ever expanding Allied bridgehead.

Above: paratroopers of the 3rd Brigade dip into their rations in the comfort of their slit trenches. (photo PAC)

Below: light and reliable, the jeep was the vehicle of choice for the airborne troops. The one shown here in LZ N on the night of June 6th is using its special trailer to carry no fewer than seven men from the Royal Ulster Rifles. (photo © IWM)

On June 7th the situation at several positions won the day before became precarious; as a result, the Canadians at Robehomme were sent to join the rest of their battalion at Le Mesnil. The 6th Airborne Armoured Reconnaissance Regiment had set up on the western side of the Bois de Bavent which was held by the 8th Parachute Battalion. That evening No. 3 Commando replaced the surviving members of the 9th Battalion at the chateau in Amfreville, these latter being sent to deploy in the woods around the chateau at St-Côme, south of Bréville. During the morning of June 7th, the 2nd Ox & Bucks took Hérouvillette and Escoville, but the latter village would fall back into the hands of the enemy that afternoon following a savage counterattack by infantry and tanks. The 1st Royal Ulster Rifles captured Longueval but was stopped short of Ste-Honorine, losing six men killed, 69 wounded, and 68 missing. At Ranville, the 13th Battalion drove off an attack led by self-propelled guns. Next door, at Bas-de-Ranville, the 12th Battalion came under a powerful attack featuring motorised infantry supported by five tanks. After three of these were destroyed, the enemy withdrew. During the evening the 12th Battalion was replaced by the 12th Devonshire which had to endure a heavy night bombardment.

The next day, June 8th, the battle for the high ground overlooking the bridgehead held by the 3rd Parachute Brigade began in earnest. With the dawn came a German attack launched by two Grenadier regiments and several tanks against the 1st Canadian Parachute Battalion. The Canadians put up fierce resistance and drove back the assault. Brigadier Hill's command post was severely threatened but was saved by reinforcements from the 9th Battalion. Along the front held by the 1st Special Service Brigade, the 45th Royal Marines Commando which had pushed inland as far as Franceville was forced to pull back to Le Hauger.

After June 6th a week of continous fighting lay in store for the Red Berets...

The 6th Airlanding Brigade was also coming under severe pressure. The 12th Devonshire were shelled continuously for several hours, while the Royal Ulsters fought off an attack on their command post and repelled a group of tanks. June 9th was marked by constant infiltrations by enemy patrols, and concentrations of infantry were observed all throughout the German lines. That evening an intense preparatory bombardment pounded the 6th Airlanding Brigade's sector from Bas-de-Ranville all the way to Hérouvillette. The following morning, the Germans let loose an assault along a front extending from Le Plein to Le Mesnil with the intention of breaking through to the bridges at Ranville and Bénouville. At Bois de Mont, the 9th Parachute Battalion, down to 170 men all told, drove back several attacks throughout the day, losing and retaking the chateau at St-Côme while inflicting heavy losses on the enemy. The Germans also tried to work a force made up of infantry and armour in between the 9th Battalion and the Canadian battalion to the south.

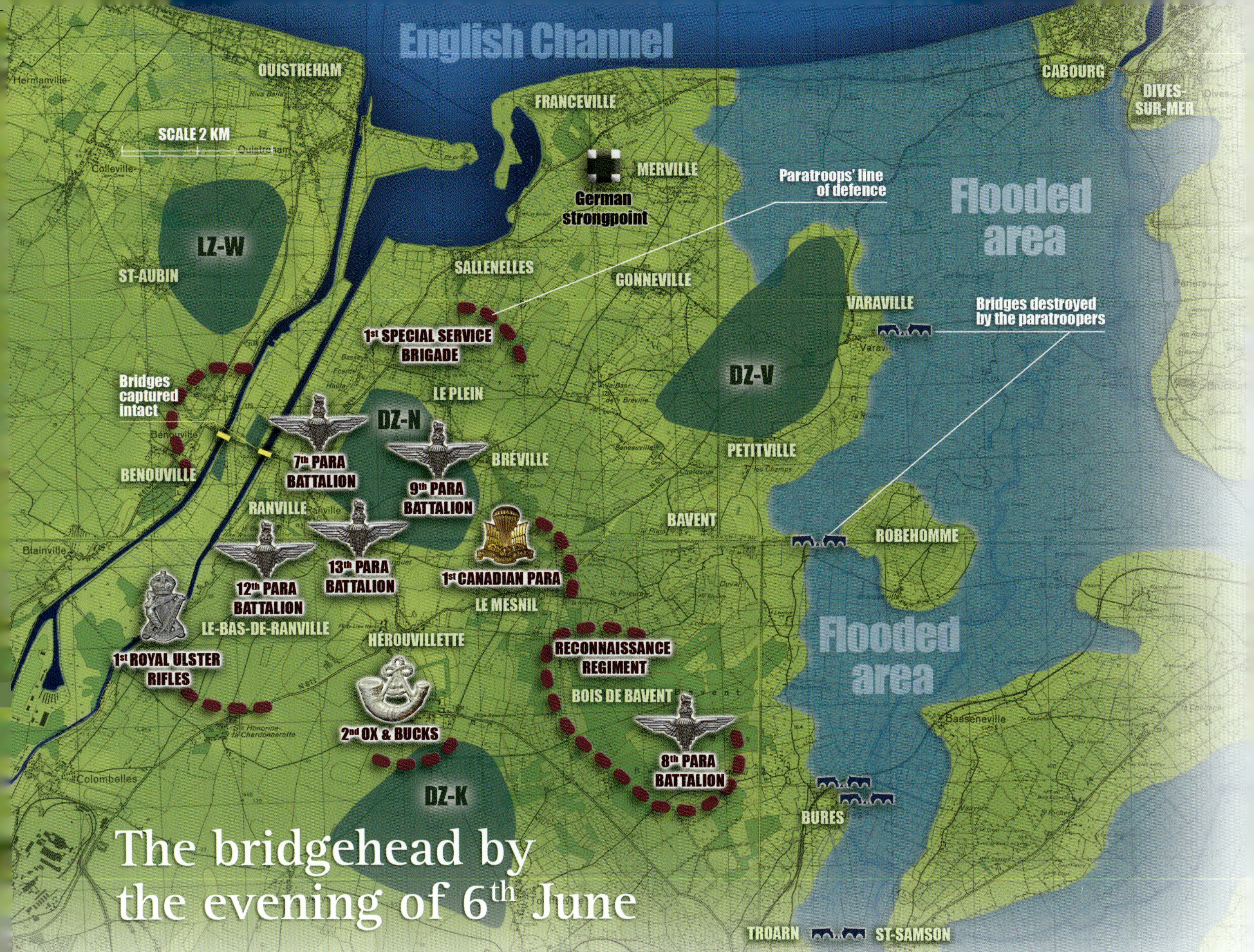

The bridgehead by the evening of 6th June

The effective combination of the two parachute battalions' machine guns and the powerful 6" guns of HMS Arethusa, providing fire support off Sword Beach, wrought great damage on the German force and denied its hopes of a breakthrough.

At Le Plein and Le Hauger, held by No. 6 and No. 4 Commandos respectively, the Germans were likewise driven back with heavy losses. Still, the enemy infantry succeeded in slipping through at Bréville and moving towards LZ V while using wrecked gliders as cover. From their positions at Ranville the paratroopers of the 13th Battalion blocked the enemy's path to the bridges; reinforced by two companies from the 7th Battalion and Sherman tanks from the 13th/18th Hussars, they showed good discipline in allowing the Germans to approach within short range before opening fire. Here, too, the German attack was shattered and the enemy losses were considerable. The survivors fell back towards the woods at Mariquet under pursuit from the paratroopers who closed in with a bayonet charge. The 13th Battalion took seventy-three prisoners. The day after, the 6th Airborne Division and the 1st Special Service Brigade which had been maintaining the defence of the Orne bridgehead for five days received welcome reinforcement from the 51st Highland Division which arrived to take over the southern flank. One of the Scottish regiments, the 5th Black Watch, relieved the 9th Battalion at the chateau St-Côme and made an attack on Bréville. To their misfortune, the enemy mortars and machine guns wrought carnage among the Highlanders who had to fall back on the chateau and mount a frantic defence against the Germans attacking through the woods. The Black Watch lost possession of the chateau itself the next day but continued to resist from an outbuilding and the surrounding woods. Otway's 9th Battalion was under heavy attack at the same time, the situation becoming so desperate that the commanding officer applied to 3rd Brigade's headquarters for reinforcements. The reinforcement was carried out by 'C' Company of the Canadian battalion whose assistance made it possible for the 9th Battalion to withdraw and at the same time to recapture the chateau at St-Côme. Still on the 12th of June, General Gale sent in an attack to capture Bréville and eradicate once and for all the threat posed by the enemy forces based there. The assault would be led by the 12th Parachute Battalion, 'D' Company of the Devonshire Regiment, and the 22nd Independent Company. Tanks from the 13th/18th Hussars and the divisional artillery of the 51st Highlanders would support the attack. The artillery barrage, however, began with a terrible misfire. The first shells struck a group of high-ranking officers gathered to watch the progress of the battle. The toll was steep – Lieutenant-Colonel "Johnny" Johnson, commander of the 12th Parachute Battalion, and Major John Bampfylde, in charge of 'D' Company of the 12th Devonshire, were killed, while Lord Lovat and Brigadier Kindersley, commander of the 6th Airlanding Brigade, were badly wounded. The attack itself was a grim affair for both battalions involved. They crossed the No Man's Land between their start line and Bréville under heavy fire from German mortars and self-propelled guns. When the paratroopers and the Devons were finally masters of the ruins that were once Bréville, 162 men had lost their lives, a total offset by the 77 Germans killed in the village. During the night, pathfinders from the 22nd Independent Company and a tank troop from the 13th/18th Hussars came up to reinforce the position. When day came, the Royal Ulsters relieved the exhausted survivors of the Bréville battle.

So ended the battle for the high ground ringing the bridgehead. After a week of intermittent fighting the red and green berets, ably supported by the Highlanders to the south, held control of the area. The 4th Special Service Brigade added to the reinforcements on June 11th. The enclave east of the Orne would from now on serve as a build-up zone for the divisions slated to take part in Operations Goodwood, Totalize, and Tractable in July and August. The 51st Highland Division left the area to take part in the latter two offensives. On August 8th Belgian and Dutch brigades were committed to the 6th Airborne's sector. The fighting changed character as mortar bombardments alternated with aggressive patrolling, ambushes, snipers, and booby-traps of all kinds. Mosquitoes abounded and tormented the combatants; but fortunately spells out of the line were arranged in various rear areas. One of these rest areas, however, was to become the scene of tragedy at the end of July when a German bomber in distress crashed onto a house in Ouistreham which was sheltering paratroopers relaxing out the line. Twenty-two of them were killed.

The matter of replacements became pressing during the campaign. In mid July, six hundred men were attached to the 6th Airborne Division to fill the void in its ranks. Coming for the most part from disbanded infantry units, 450 of these men went into the depleted parachute battalions without having earned qualification as paratroopers.

Bréville after the battle. The wrecks of two German Marder III (self-propelled tank destroyers) can be seen. In the foreground is a 20 mm Flak (anti-aircraft) gun. (photo Pegasus Memorial /DR)

The Windak Smock worn by Bob Sheridan, one of the very rare examples preserved of this high quality item.

The letters A.M. on the tab are a reminder that the initial contract with the firm making the smocks was approved by the Air Ministry.

Two large pockets made of denim fabric were added on the lower back of the smock.

Captain Robert Sheridan's Jump-Jacket

Bob Sheridan, a staff officer with the Royal Ulster Rifles, opted for a "Windak Smock," a jump-jacket of superior quality. This type of jacket opened in full at the front, and the strap that passed between the legs to prevent the rush of air from billowing the jacket during the jump could then be buttoned at the back. This brand of smock was mainly worn by senior officers.

Strangely, the covering of the left rear pocket was sewn on backwards, leaving the inner lining open to view.

The Military Medal of Rifleman Charles Feeney. On June 7th, Feeney took part in the attack on Ste-Honorine. When his platoon was pinned down by enemy fire, Feeney covered his comrades with smoke grenades. He remained behind on his own under a rain of mortar bombs to help a wounded man. His courageous conduct earned the twenty-year old soldier the medal shown. Sadly, on August 24th, he was killed at Trouville.

Original beret worn by a member of the Royal Ulster Rifles.

1st Royal Ulster Rifles

The Royal Ulster Rifles regiment was the only one in the British Army to have its two battalions take part in the D-Day landings. The 1st Battalion came in by glider on the night of June 5th-6th, while the 2nd Battalion landed on the morning of June 6th at Sword Beach with the 3rd British Division. The regiment contained a high proportion of Irishmen, many of whom were volunteers from the neutral Republic of Ireland who bravely came forward to fight against the Nazis.

Sergeant J. Cramer, 1st Royal Ulsters Rifles. The insignia opposite was the one that can be seen on his lower right sleeve. It was a non-official brevet worn by glider-borne troops, in this case on the green backing of the Rifles.
Below, his copy of the word and phrases book for use by British soldiers in Germany.

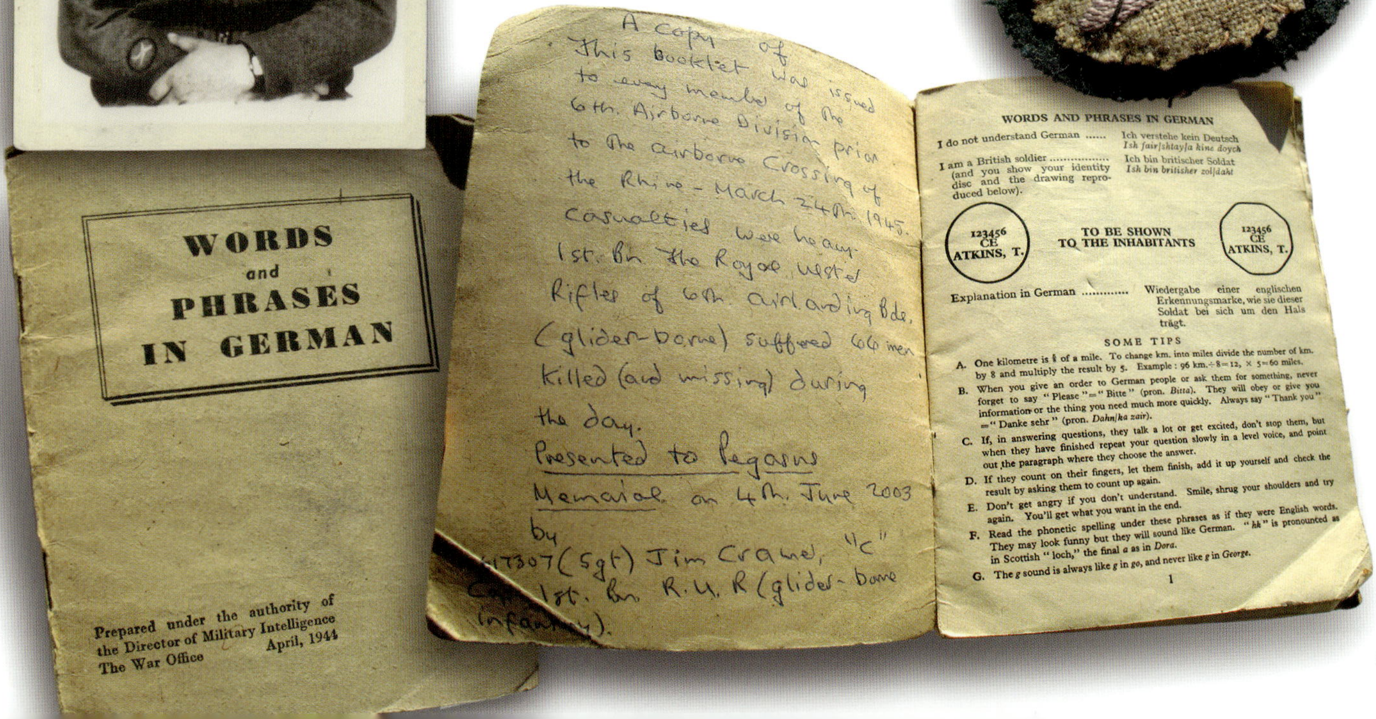

© The objects shown on this page come from the collections of the Pegasus Memorial in Ranville.

The Denison Smock worn by Captain Webber, donated to the Pegasus Memorial.

Captain John Webber's Denison Smock

In the early hours of June 6th, 'A' Company of the 7th Parachute Battalion found itself in a difficult pass. Its commander, Major Nigel Taylor, was out of action, as were the rest of its officers with the exception of Captain Webber. Although wounded himself, Webber took charge of the company which was surrounded and without means of communication. For seventeen hours he inspired his men as they confronted a larger enemy force supported by self-propelled guns. The company was safely withdrawn at the end of the day. Webber received the Military Cross, although some felt that he deserved the Victoria Cross.

The paratrooper's insignia, at that time sewn on the right sleeve.

The pipe that Captain Webber took with him in battle.

A. Brown's oversmock

This large sleeveless smock went over the paratrooper's webbing to prevent the parachute cords from tangling with his equipment during the jump. Once he landed, the oversmock allowed him to get out of his harness easily and was left behind with his parachute. The one shown here belonged to a paratrooper named A. Brown and was found at Touffreville. The blue circle within the white border was a symbol enabling paratroopers to identify men from their own unit as they regrouped in the drop zone.

A paratrooper's name and army number on the inside of the oversmock.

This fine example of a Denison Smock was found in the Pays d'Auge several decades after the war. It was worn by a lumberjack...

T187984

Jeremy H. Barkway, 6th A.A.R.R. This tank crewman who came from the 3rd King's Own Hussars disembarked from a Hamilcar on D-Day as commander of a Tetrarch tank. He went through the entire Normandy campaign and on into the Battle of the Bulge and the invasion of Germany.
(photo Pegasus Memorial / DR)

Operation Paddle

The pursuit to the Seine, August 17th-27th, 1944

On August 7th, while the Canadians were advancing towards Falaise and the Americans were about to break through at Avranches, the Allied High Command anticipated a German withdrawal to the Seine River. In view of this, Lieutenant-General John Crocker, commander of 1st British Corps, ordered Major-General Gale to prepare his troops to undertake pursuit of the enemy in the event of a retirement in this sector.

These two colour photos taken in August 1944 offer us a rare view of some of the eight Cromwell tanks received at the beginning of the month by 'A' Squadron of the 6th A.A.R.R. The red berets and Denison Smocks worn by the crews are clearly visible; they reflect their pride in being members of the airborne's armoured regiment.
(photos PAC)

A general advance by 1st Corps would proceed along the coast and through the Pays d'Auge in the direction of the River Seine and its estuary. This presented Gale with several problems. A quick advance would require suitable transport, and yet the 6th Airborne Division and the Special Service Brigades were far from being completely motorised formations. The bridging equipment available to the airborne units was insufficient to cope with the number of watercourses running across its route; and furthermore, Gale could be sure of limited artillery support at best.

The long march of the paratroopers and commandos to the Seine Estuary.

Two main paths of advance were marked out on the basis on their practicability. The 6th Airlanding Brigade, reinforced by Belgian and Dutch brigades, both motorised and operational, would advance along the coastal zone, while the other units would proceed mainly along the route linking Troarn with Pont-Audemer.

The general quiet along the 6th Airborne's front on August 16th gave rise to thoughts that the enemy had taken his leave. Towards 20h00, prisoner interrogations indicated that the Wehrmacht's 346th Infantry Division was retreating past Troarn. During the night patrols by paratroopers and commandos confirmed that the enemy had abandoned his positions.

The next day, at 03h00, Operation Paddle began. The 3rd Parachute Brigade set off across the wooded terrain and reached Bures where the sappers fashioned a raft to pass the 6-pounder guns from one bank to the other. At the next watercourse, the Muance, a makeshift crossing was installed for jeeps by extending an old railway embankment. The commandos of the 1st Special Service Brigade took Bavent, Varaville, and Robehomme during the day of August 17th. The 8th Parachute Battalion took Goustranville that night after hard fighting but could not prevent the destruction of the bridge over the Dives Canal. On the coast the Belgian brigade under Colonel Jean-Baptiste Piron took Salenelles and entered Franceville. The 12th Devonshire took Gonneville in the morning; on the other hand, the Royal Ulster Rifles met stout resistance in the outskirts of Cabourg and pulled back to Le Home for the night. The next day, Major-General Gale ordered the Irishmen to keep up the pressure on Cabourg without mounting a costly attack since the weight of the division's effort would be concentrated on the Troarn-Dozulé path of advance. Brigadier Hill's 3rd Parachute Brigade was to cross the Dives Canal and secure its crossing points so as to allow the 5th Brigade to move through at a good pace and take Putot-en-Auge. Gale wished to get his men away from what he called *"the island,"* in other words, the constricted zone between the Dives and the canal that was fully exposed to enemy artillery and controlled from the heights of Dozulé and Putot.

Above, on August 28th, 1944, Troopers C. Davies and C. Walker arrive in Pont-Audemer on board their captured German SDKFZ (special motorised vehicle). Using the anti-aircraft gun mounted on the back of this half-track the two men were credited with shooting down two enemy fighters. (photo IWM)

Below, the arrival of the paratroopers in Beuzeville on the morning of August 26th. In the photo on the right, the paratrooper in the middle has somehow got hold of a Mark II helmet marked with the white band designating members of the Beach Groups. (photos P. Hémery / DR)

Of the four possible crossing sites identified by the British three had been destroyed, although one could still be used by infantry. The fourth was seized intact by the 1st Canadian Parachute Battalion which immediately christened it "Canada Bridge." The German forces that opposed the paratroopers in Operation Paddle did not give the impression of a main body intending to halt an offensive; it was far more important to the Germans to play for time by controlling strategic points – a crossroads, a road, a piece of high ground – for as long as possible. Once across the canal, the 9th Battalion captured the railway station at Dozulé in the early hours of August 19th, not without paying a heavy toll to the enemy's artillery. During the day, the 12th Battalion took Putot-en-Auge, but when the 13th Battalion threw itself into an attack on Hill 13 it was driven back with not inconsiderable losses. The feature was taken the next night by the 48th Royal Marines Commando. With a view to capturing the high ground at Brucourt, north of Putot-en-Auge, Brigadier Derek Mills-Robert slipped his 1st Special Service Brigade between the enemy lines. This bold stroke achieved the desired result and gave the commandos control of the heights overlooking the Dives. Mindful of keeping the advance going without getting bogged down in costly struggles in well-defended towns, Gale gave orders to bypass Dozulé and Cabourg. The seaside resort did fall to the Belgians on August 20th and Dozulé was abandoned the next day but not before much of it was partially put to the torch by the Germans. Gale then sent the Belgian Brigade and the other motorised units at his disposal, the Dutch "Prinses Irene" Brigade and the 6th Airborne Armoured Reconnaissance Regiment, to explore the enemy positions around Pont-l'Évêque. The reconnaissance unit ran into strong defences at Annebault which could seriously impede the 6th Airborne's progress, and so the 8th and 9th Battalions attacked the village which was finally taken after a lengthy, hard fight. On the morning of the 22nd, the 5th Parachute Brigade carried on its advance from Annebault; the 13th Battalion was ordered to besiege Pont-l'Évêque while the 12th Battalion secured the approaches to the village from the south by taking control of the heights at St-Julien. The first stage in this action went rather well for the 12th Battalion which advanced under cover of smoke shells fired by the 150th and 191st Field Regiments of the Royal Artillery. Unfortunately, when the smoke screen evaporated, the enemy machine guns and artillery stopped the paratroopers in their tracks. The forward elements had to retrace their steps for lack of ammunition and the bulk of the battalion used the dark of night to cover their retirement. In the town itself, the 13th Battalion crossed the first of the two bridges spanning the Touques River but the Germans retained firm control over the road leading to the second. Four Cromwell tanks from the reconnaissance regiment lent what help they could, but they could not get over the river and one of them was set ablaze by a 20 mm gun. As at Dozulé, the Germans withdrew after leaving much of the town a smoking ruin. Still on the 22nd, the Royal Ulster Rifles and the Belgians liberated Deauville and Trouville; the 1st Belgian Brigade then assisted the 6th Airlanding Brigade in its advance to the coast. Towns and villages were liberated one by one, usually after brief rear-guard actions, until the advance reached Honfleur on August 25th.

Further south, after going around Pont-l'Évêque (which the 5th Parachute Brigade was in the process of clearing), the 1st Special Service Brigade spearheaded the advance all the way to the outskirts of Beuzeville where it stumbled upon determined resistance. The 4th Special Service Brigade and the 3rd Parachute Brigade then joined the battle unfolding around Beuzeville that lasted well into the night. Cromwell tanks of the Armoured Reconnaissance Regiment and elements of the Belgian Brigade added their support. Early in the morning of August 26th, paratroopers of the 3rd Brigade finally entered Beuzeville which the Germans had evacuated during the night. The evening of the previous day, Major-General Gale had received an order from Crocker to halt his division in order to leave the way clear for the 49th Infantry Division, particularly the route to Pont-Audemer. Gale, however, felt that his troops were better placed to take the town before the Germans blew the bridges over the Risle River. He therefore ignored the order and sent the 7th Parachute Battalion, along with elements from the Belgian and Dutch brigades and the 22nd Independent Parachute Company, on a forced march to Pont-Audemer. At the end of a remarkable race against time, the first Allied soldiers entered the town just as the bridges went sailing into the air.

After taking control of the south bank of the Seine Estuary, the 6th Airborne saw its part in the Battle of Normandy come to an end. As of August 28th, the division began to assemble at Arromanches and embarked for England on September 4th. At the end of eighty-two days of fighting, the 6th Airborne Division had lost 821 men killed, 2,709 wounded, and 927 missing.

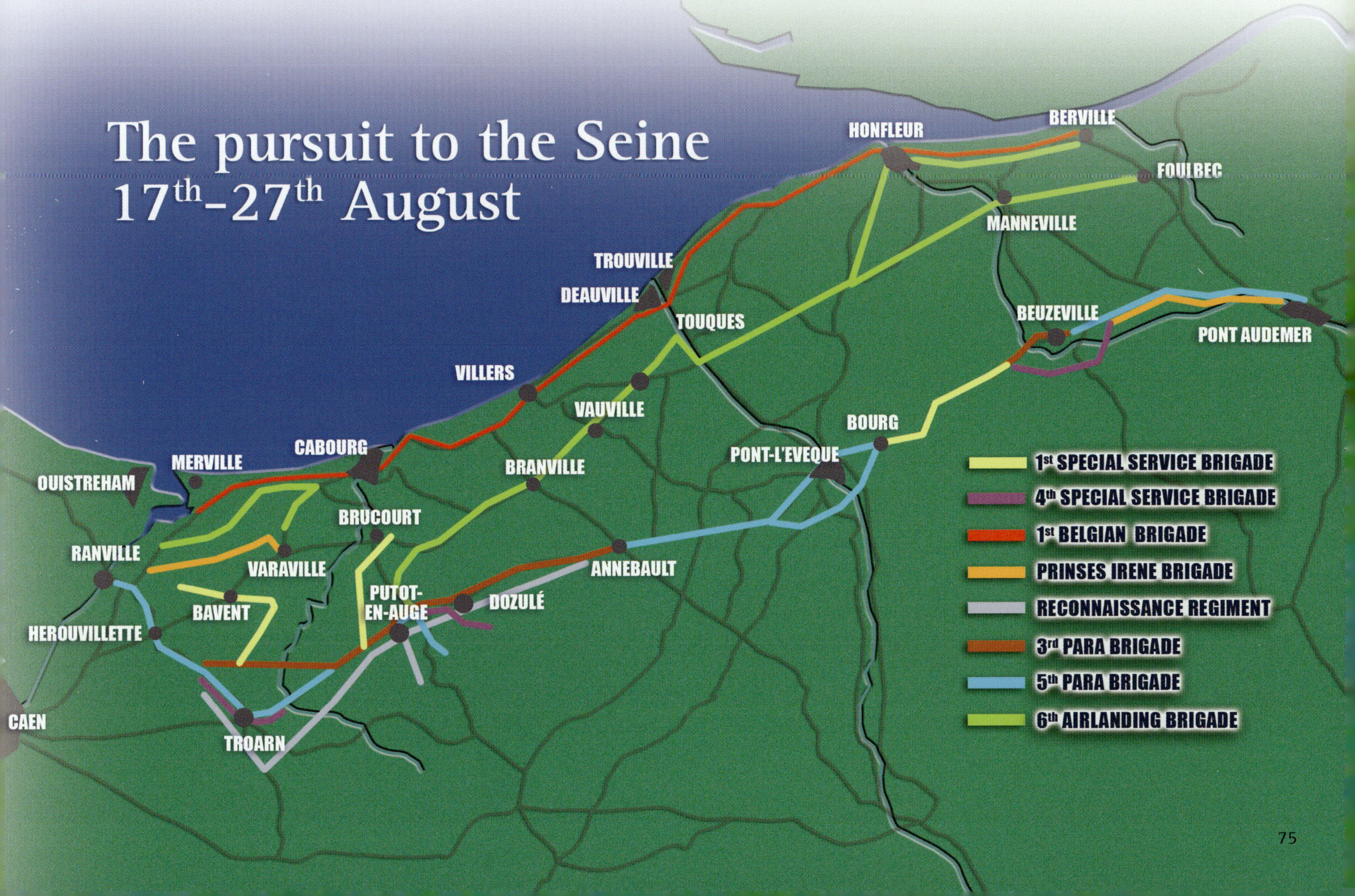

Lance Corporal Waters's medals, from left to right: 1939-45 Star, France & Germany Star, Defence Medal 1939-45, War Medal, and General Service Medal 1918-64.

Lance Corporal Waters here wears an interesting combination of insignia: shoulder title of the Royal Armoured Corps, worn by tank crews; the Pegasus emblem and the Airborne patch. On his beret he has the cap badge of his original unit, the North Staffordshire Regiment.(photo Pegasus Memorial / DR)

His uniform, an exceptional example of the ones worn by the tank crews of the Airborne Division with their shoulder titles and cap badges of the RAC.

Two sets of identity discs, one of pressed fibre worn by Lance Corporal Waters in Europe, the other of rot-proof metal that he received for use in the Far East.

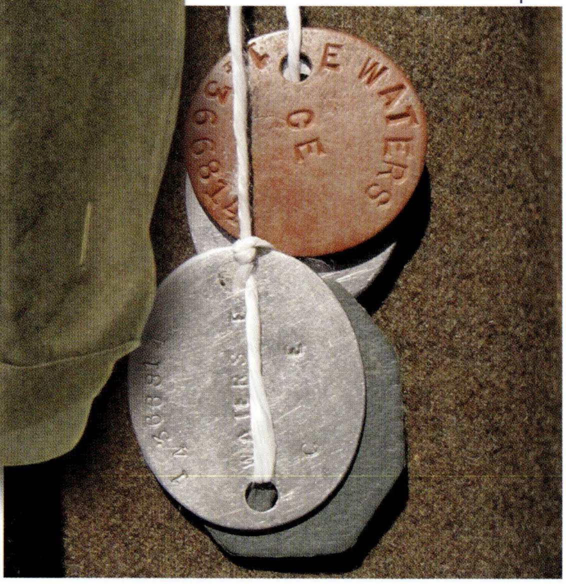

An extraordinary cap badge fashioned by Sergeant Steve Tomkinson. This unique example symbolically blends the Royal Armoured Corps, with its mailed fist emblem in the centre, and the Airborne forces, represented by the spreading wings of the parachute badge. Below is a cigarette box made out of plexiglass from a tank.

A Cromwell tank of the 6th A.A.R.R. rolling through Normandy in August 1944. (photo PAC)

Sergeant Steve Tomkinson commanded one of the Tetrarch tanks that landed at Ranville on the evening of June 6th. Unfortunately a Hamilcar glider crashed into his tank and badly damaged it. (photo Pegasus Memorial / DR)

The 6th A.A.R.R.
The tank crews with the red beret

The 6th Airborne Division was the only one with its own armoured reconnaissance regiment. This distinction was a source of great pride which the men in this unit displayed on their uniforms where the insignia of the Royal Armoured Corps and the Airborne Division were mounted side by side.

Another of the clever Sergeant's masterpieces, this one a small-scale model of a Tetrarch that he made in the field out of tin cans he had salvaged.

© The objects shown on these pages come from the collections of the Pegasus Memorial in Ranville.

On August 30th, 1944, the talented T.D. Hendry of the 225th Parachute Field Ambulance sketched this timbered building, typical of the region, that served as temporary lodging for a mortar platoon. In the margins he depicted a Sten Mark V, a Bren Carrier, and an allegory of the liberation, symbolised by a hammer smashing chains on an anvil.
(© Collection Pegasus Memorial)

A Belgian motorcyclist from the "Brigade Piron" photographed at Beuzeville at the end of August 1944. (photos P. Hémery / DR)

The Seine Estuary
Traces of a campaign's dénouement

In the last week of August 1944, paratroopers, commandos, Belgians and Dutch reached the Seine Estuary. For the 6th Airborne Division and the 1st Special Service Brigade, the Normandy campaign ended here. In the zone between Beuzeville, Honfleur, and Pont-Audemer, Major-General Gale's men would enjoy a few days of rest as they awaited the journey to Arromanches and from there by ship back to the United Kingdom.

In the village of Ablon, Gaston Petit, a young member of the French Resistance (FFI), stopped a jeep driven by Belgian soldiers to warn them of snipers in the area. Since he wished to dislodge the enemy sharpshooters himself, one of the Belgians rummaged around in the vehicle and handed him this captured German semi-automatic rifle (a Walther G41). The young man was unable to carry out his plan, however, which undoubtedly saved his life.

This Sten Mark V machine-pistol, a model specially designed for airborne troops, was found at Honfleur in the 1980s.

The weapon preserves the traces of green stripes, a sign that it was camouflaged at the time it was used.

"'He's lucky to be alive,' said a paratrooper bitterly."

This illustration taken from the newspaper shown below evokes the exploits of the paratroopers on June 6th.

Also found at Honfleur during the 1980s, this June 9th issue of the Daily Express contains an article by reporter Leonard Mosley who jumped with the British paratroopers on D-Day.

2

DAILY EXPRESS FRIDAY JUNE 9, 1944

CINEMA THEATRES

DAILY EXPRESS
Opinion

Waiting for it

PATIENCE has always stood high among the war-making virtues; and never higher than now.

Fortunately the British people have plenty of it. They will understand why Mr. Churchill does not want to make daily or regular speeches on the invasion.

It will be days and weeks—some say up to four or five weeks—before the people at home will see the great pattern of events emerging.

Look back

TO get a steady and a ...

... To the public sitting at home a military collapse comes with the sudden shock of a thunderclap.

But the surprise itself has actually been built up in months of arduous training and preparation.

Often in the time of preparation there seemed to be a stalemate or worse. In Russia, Stalin's armies fell back and back to the gates of Leningrad and Moscow. Then came Stalingrad to uphold and glorify Russian faith and patience.

They waited

IN North Africa there was the retreat back to Alamein. Again the wait-...

WILLIAM HICKEY
VICE VERSA

COINCIDENTALLY, William the Conqueror came from Caen in Normandy. He founded the castle there in 1066 for the very purpose of invading England.

Furthermore Roger de Montgomery, who is said to have led the Norman right at the Battle of Hastings, took his name from Montgomery, his ancestral home in the Department of Calvados in Normandy of which Caen is the capital.

Roger in turn gave his name to the town in Wales, where he built himself a castle in 1072. And the present General Montgomery traces his descent right back to Norman times and to the eleventh-century invader. And ...

The General said:—
'Only a fool would invade in bad weather—well I'm going to'
—and we did it

by Leonard Mosley, *Combined Press Reporter*

"I believe that the things they have done are almost solely and completely responsi-...

BEHIND THE ATLANTIC WALL.

THIS is one of those stories that will have ...

I believe that the things they have done are almost solely and completely responsible for the great success our invasion has had so far in this sector.

Our job as an airborne force was to silence a vital coastal battery, which if still in operation might have blown our ships to bits as they came to the shore. We silenced it.

And our other just as vital job was to secure two important bridges over the canal and river north of Caen, to prevent them from being blown up, and to hold them against all comers until the main armies arrived. We are still holding them. They are still intact.

So let us begin this story as I emplaned in "C for Charlie," a great black bomber, at 11.20 p.m., and we took our place in the taxi-ing line of planes that stretched from one end to the other of one of the biggest airfields in Britain.

There were Lancashire men, Yorkshire men and Northumbrians mostly in the "stick" of paratroopers, and except for me they were the beefiest bunch of armed men I have ever seen. They knew their job and they knew how difficult it was going to be.

Preceding them by half ...

"A roaring that rapidly grew to a thunderous roll."

plane as it coasted in and down to the dropping zone. And we were scared by it—until the red light flashed before our eyes, then swiftly changed to green, and we were all madly shuffling down the hole and jumping into space.

I looked as I twisted down for the church I had been told to spy for a landmark, and for the wood where we were later going to rendezvous as a fighting force. But the wind had caught me, and was whisking me east. Faster and faster I twisted, and I had to wrestle with my straps to get me straight.

... figures, and they were coming towards me and I could see that they were carrying guns.

What might have happened is one of those "ifs" of my private history—only there was a crash of Sten gunfire instead and both men crumpled up not 15 yards from me. Into the field stealthily came five men to challenge me—and I was with our own paratroopers again.

A drink of wine

FOR two long, weary hours we wandered the country. We hid from German ...

... on rocks and careered into still undestroyed poles.

But it was hard to restrain the impulse to cheer, for, out of every glider, men were pouring, and jeeps, and anti-tank guns and field guns—and we knew that even if Nazi tanks did come now we could hold ...

...bers like bees

... now, as a faint glow began to appear in the sky, our eyes turned ...wards. For ... that ...nderous ...ed.

... climax of ...asion was ... Here were ... swarming in like bees ... coastal defences ... up before our ...

And what a sight it was! ... two miles away, ... of explosions lifted us off the ground. Soon the sky was lit with a green and purple glow from the burning Nazi dumps.

As dawn came I moved across country through Nazi patrols to get nearer to the coast. Wherever we moved there were traces of our airborne invasion. Emptied containers, still burning their signal lights, were scattered in fields and orchards. Wrecked gliders littered the ground, some of them splintered to matchwood. There were parachutes lying everywhere.

In the orchard where I had landed we saw a shape in a tree and went up to it. It was a man who had jumped shortly before me in my stick. He was beyond help—Nazi machine gunners had seen to that. But the ripped body of a young Nazi a few yards away showed that he had not died unavenged. It was hazardous going, because Nazi patrols were numerous in this area.

Eventually we reached high ground overlooking the coast, and waited until our watches showed 7.15 ...

said. "We have waited a long time for the hour of liberation."

There were children playing in the streets, unmindful of the war only a few yards away.

Inside headquarters you could hardly hear men talking for the sound of shells, bombs and bullets dropping all around us. But the general was calm. "Everything is fine," he said. "It's going exactly to plan. Don't worry, we'll hold them."

It was at his suggestion I made my way back to the bridges to contact one of our units holding the bridgehead on the other side until the seaborne forces arrived. It was a hazardous journey.

Every yard of the way smelled of death, for Germans and British lay in the mud side by side where they had fought in darkness for possession of bridges. Battered on buttresses were wrecks of three of the gliders which had made the hazardous first descent and captured spans intact.

Revenge

HALF-WAY over I came across a Nazi soldier groaning from a wound in his stomach. "He's lucky to be alive," said a paratrooper bitterly. "He's one of the snipers. He shot three of my pals this morning, but we got him finally."

Across the canal bridge snipers' bullets were zipping like fireflies, but the risk you had to take crossing it was negligible compared with what the paratroop battalion holding the bridgehead were facing. Nazi counter-attacks were coming in every few minutes. A shower of mortar and shell fire was concentrated terror.

But these Lancashire lads were holding on, and though their numbers were growing hourly smaller they would continue to hold on. Until well after noon we were still ...ed. The unit fought on until gradually all opposition from the north-west ceased and to their delight and relief a ...

HONFLEUR
Fbg. St. Léonard
Fiquefleur
-Equainville
Joble
la Rivière
-St. Sauveur
Fatouville
-Grestain
les Londes
St.-Pierre-du-Val
les Varets
Buquet
la Bruyère
Ablon
la Chiais
la Terrerie
le Mesnil-Ferry
la Bigrerie
les Parquets
Castel
la Croix Hauton
Hunieres
Fourneville
Lieu du Val
Montchaudet
Bonnemare
les Bourdons
la Roche
le Lion
les Pognons
Bellelonde
BEUZEVILLE
Côte de Ransue
la Roquerie
Vallee
Beaumousse
les Bottentuits
la Beaudeulnière
Rue d'Enfer

Page at left, overlaid on a map of the time: British cutlery found at the positions held by the 46th Royal Marines Commando, south of Beuzeville. The British belt was found by Michel Delamarre near a field hospital at Carbec. The regulation "Mug" was also found in the trail left by the 46th Royal Marines. The Bren gun magazine was found in a farm building belonging to M. Delamarre.

This Bren magazine was found in a barn near Beuzevillle.

© All items from private collections

Cap-badge of the Prinses Irene Brigade given to a young inhabitant of Beuzeville by a Dutch soldier.

Remnants of the battle for Beuzeville

Over two days in late August of 1944 the paratroopers and commandos fought their last pitched battles of the Normandy campaign around Beuzeville. Although the village was spared the worst, the inhabitants found that the outskirts had become the scene of bitter fighting. The Allied soldiers killed were reverently collected and buried. The field ambulances came to provide emergency treatment to a multitude of wounded men. As a succession of Allied units passed through Beuzeville, a local photographer captured these moments for posterity. After the soldiers left, the images remained, and so did the bits and pieces which the passage of time would transform into relics.

A paratrooper poses for a photograph in Beuzeville on August 26th, 1944. He is equipped with a bandolier with seven pouches holding Sten gun magazines and is wearing, interestingly, a Mark II helmet....

Here an airborne jeep is going by, bedecked with a flag and towing its trailer. The whole contraption is overloaded with paratroopers who, oddly enough, are also wearing Mark II helmets instead of their special paratroop models.

In the same spot, other paratroopers arrive to the cheers of the locals.
(photos P. Hémery / DR)

The beret of Sergeant Hubert van Roelen, 1st Belgian Artillery Battery, seconded as an artillery spotter to the 2nd Motorised Unit.

Sergeant van Roelen's decorations: Croix de Guerre 1939-45 (France); Croix des Evadés 1940-45 (Belgium); 1939-45 Star and France-Germany Star (Great Britain).

Insignia showing Sergeant van Roelen's nationality and unit. The insignia of the Belgian Brigade is of the second model, approved for use in late 1944.

Original battle dress worn by Sergeant van Roelen.

1st Belgian Brigade

Towards the end of 1942 Major Jean-Baptiste Piron took command of the 1st Belgian Independent Grouping, a unit made up of Belgian soldiers who had come to Britain in 1940 and of expatriate Belgians from all over the world. It grew in size as an independent, mobile formation endowed with its own reconnaissance and artillery units. In 1944 the Grouping became a Brigade, commonly known as the "Brigade Piron" after its commander, now a Lieutenant-Colonel. The Belgians arrived in Normandy at the beginning of August 1944 and were placed under the authority of the 6th Airborne Division. Major-General Gale would put this highly mobile brigade composed of seasoned combatants to good use. The Belgian Brigade would provide valuable assistance to the paratroopers during Operation Paddle and liberate a good deal of the Norman coast. In four weeks of fighting the Brigade lost 27 men killed and had 87 wounded.

Private René Vereecken belonged to the machine gun platoon of the 3rd Motorised Company of the Piron Brigade. After volunteering for a patrol, he was mortally wounded at Deauville on August 24th, 1944.

Belgians and Dutch with 6th Airborne Division

In August of 1944, in addition to his red berets, Major-General Gale had two units of commandos (the 1st and 4th Special Service Brigades) under his command, as well as two brigades of Belgian and Dutch volunteers. These men, fighting for the Allies and for the freedom of their countries, provided much needed manpower to a division that had suffered mounting losses ever since June 6th.

Cap badge of the "Prinses Irene Brigade", fittingly mounted on an orange backing.

The "Prinses Irene Brigade"

Also called by the British 1st Royal Netherland Brigade, this unit was created in 1941 and filled its ranks with Dutch refugees in Britain and with volunteers of Dutch background from South Africa, North America, and the Netherlands' colonies in southeast Asia.

The Dutch brigade arrived in Normandy on August 6th, 1944 and went into battle for the first time a few days later at the chateau St-Côme. During Operation Paddle, the Dutch followed a line of advance centred on Dozulé - Pont-l'Évêque; after August 24th the brigade came under the command of the 5th Parachute Brigade which employed the Dutch in reconnaissance operations around Beuzeville and Pont-Audemer.

British Mark II of the "Prinses Irene Brigade" helmet with the emblem of the Free Dutch Forces.

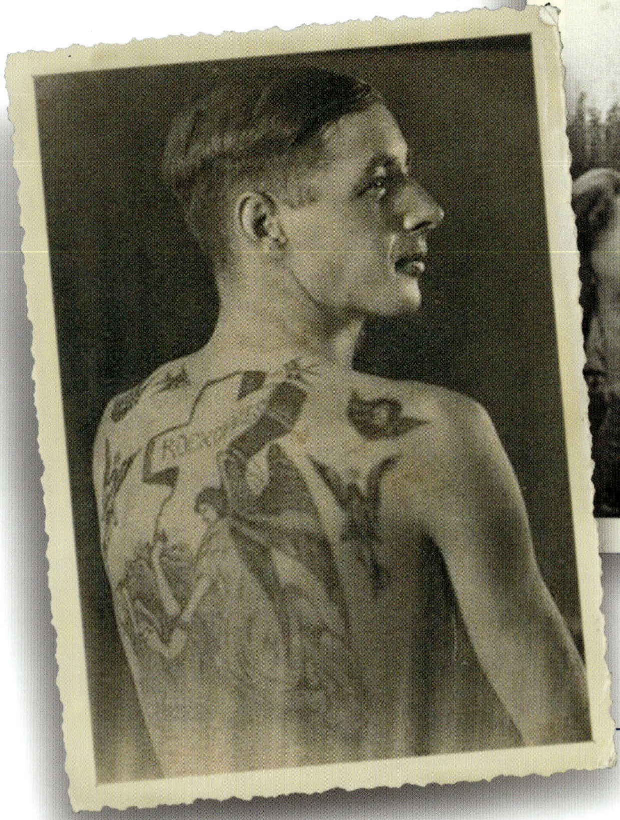

The tattoos on McIlhargey's back. On the arm of the Cross the title of the famous hymn "Rock of Ages" is inscribed.

In India during the 1930s, four Cameronians show off their new tattoos. McIlhargey is third from the left, with a Bengal tiger tattooed on his stomach.

Lance-Sergeant C. R. McIlhargey

Born in Glasgow on November 11th, 1915, Charles Rutherford McIlhargey fit the image of the British soldier immortalised by Rudyard Kipling. Enlisted in the Cameronians (Scottish Rifles), he served in India during the 1930s. From there he brought back a spectacular set of tattoos which, coupled with his larger than life character, gave him a certain aura in the eyes of his comrades.

Charles McIlhargey was an early volunteer for the parachute battalion. An experienced soldier tried and tested in India, he was a typical product of that environment, rough and tumble but with a dependability that reassured his comrades and officers. The reminiscences of others paint him as a man with a taste for solitude, yet a splendid comrade in arms and a bit of a joker. It would also seem that his blunt talk and refusal to let anyone walk all over him made him moving up and down the rank. It was with a Lance-Sergeant's stripes that he jumped into Normandy on the night of June 5th-6th with 'C' Company of the 8th Parachute Battalion. Throughout the campaign he showed himself to be an efficient NCO and a formidable soldier who distinguished himself on several patrols. He would get right up to the enemy positions and bring back valuable information, even bringing back three prisoners on one occasion. On August 25th, while leading another patrol during the fierce fighting around Beuzeville, McIlhargey was wounded at the same time as Private Robert Box. Both paratroopers were captured and had their hands tied before they were taken away in a truck. Their bodies were found five days later at Vatteville-la-Rue where they had been buried after being murdered with a shot to the back of the head. The two men lie at rest today in the communal cemetery.

Charles McIlhargey here wears the insignia which preceded the later types devised for the Parachute Regiment; they replaced the "Airborne" shoulder titles and the Army Air Corps cap badges in the spring of 1943.
(All photos DR)

Battle dress blouse worn by Sergeant Eaglen at the end of the war.

Private Ted Eaglen before the invasion. Aged 19 years on D-Day, he would "celebrate" his twentieth birthday in Normandy. (photo St-Martin)

As a veteran Ted Eaglen remained faithful to the memory of his fallen comrades, returning each year to pay his respects. (photo St-Martin)

Private Ted Eaglen
A gift to a paratrooper

Ted Eaglen was serving as a private in the Northamptonshire Regiment when he volunteered for the paratroopers. Breveted in 1943, he was assigned to 'C' Company of the 8th Parachute Battalion. On the night of June 5th-6th, 1944, he was a member of an advanced party who accompanied the pathfinders of the 22nd Independent Parachute Company on Drop Zone K at 00h20. A jump into the heart of darkness..

Greeted by enemy fire as soon as they landed in Drop Zone K, the pathfinders of the 8th Battalion secured the assembly point of their unit. One German soldier was killed and another taken prisoner. It was the pathfinders' task to guide their comrades to the rendezvous point as well as to locate the gliders and help with their unloading. At 00h50, they assisted the battalion's landing which was widely dispersed. They managed to find two of the Horsas that had been heading for Drop Zone K. After June 6th the battalion took positions in the wooded areas at Bures and Bavent. Ted Eaglen spent the summer of his twentieth year in the shadows and humidity of the forest, with the mosquitoes, German mortar bombs, and reconnaissance patrols night and day, often into Troarn and Bures, seeing his comrades fall and the enemy's dead...

The young paratrooper saw each day as a reprieve. In the course of one patrol he captured a German who had used an old woman to shield himself. In gratitude for saving her, she gave him the rosary that she wore around her neck. Not being Catholic, Eaglen did not realise what the token of thanks meant until a few days later an officer explained it to him. He carried the rosary for the rest of the war.

After Normandy, Ted Eaglen fought in the Ardennes and in Germany. Wounded three times, he found the old woman's gift to be a deep source of comfort in his trials.

The rosary given to Ted Eaglen in 1944.

Display area at the Pegasus Memorial dedicated to Major Tarrant, with a model of the Chateau Bruder at Ranville.

Major R. M. Tarrant, MC
'B' Company, 13th Parachute Battalion

Born in Dorsetshire in 1913, Reginald Mowlam Tarrant was a career soldier. A lieutenant in the Dorset Regiment during the 1930s, he later served as a staff officer in British Guiana. He was promoted to captain in 1941 and volunteered for the paratroopers in 1943. He then went to the 13th Parachute Battalion and on becoming a major took command of the Headquarters Company.

Fifty minutes after midnight on June 6th, Major Tarrant parachuted into Drop Zone N. In one of his pockets he carried a small mascot, a "Raggedy Ann" doll borrowed from his young son. He took part in the capture of the German headquarters in Ranville where he found a Nazi flag that he kept as a souvenir. At the end of July he took command of 'B' Company, replacing Major G.W. Bristow who had been wounded at Le Mesnil a few days before.

When he jumped into Normandy, Major Tarrant was carrying with him his son's "Raggedy Ann" doll as a mascot.

A trophy claimed on June 6th, this flag was captured by Reggie Tarrant in the offices of the German headquarters in the Chateau Bruder, at Ranville.

Major Tarrant's sword, worn on parade.

A posthumous portrait of Major R.M. Tarrant; in it he wears the ribbon of the Military Cross awarded after his death.

Then on August 17th the 6th Airborne undertook the pursuit of the retreating enemy; by evening of the next day the 13th Parachute Battalion was at Goustranville. The 5th Brigade was to cross the Dives River in order to secure the area around Putot-en-Auge. The 19th the 12th Battalion captured the village while the 7th established a strong defensive position. The 13th Battalion passed through them to take the heights east of Putot at Hill 13. 'B' Company set off first, as Reggie Tarrant quickly conducted his men to the base of the hill and led the charge himself with fixed bayonets. Several resistance points were cleared, but the paratroopers soon found their way blocked by machine guns and ninety Germans who had just arrived to reinforce the defenders.

Although badly wounded in the stomach, Major Tarrant continued to direct his men. Despite repeated attempts the 13th Battalion could not take Hill 13. It would be the artillery of the 151st Field Regiment supporting an attack by the 48th Royal Marine Commando which would prove too much for the German defenders on the night of August 19th. Major Tarrant died of his wounds in a field hospital on August 28th, at the age of 31, and lies at rest in Douvres-la-Délivrande War Cemetery. He received a posthumous Military Cross in recognition of his courageous leadership at Hill 13.

Major Tarrant's medals. From the left, his posthumous Military Cross, awarded for his actions at the head of 'B' Company on August 19th, 1944.

Corporal William Henry Lambley, 2nd Ox & Bucks. This veteran of D-Day died in Holland at the age of 24, on February 8th, 1945. (photo IWM)

The Battle of the Bulge
and the operations along the River Maas

On December 16th, 1944, Hitler made one last throw of the dice to defeat the Allied armies in the west. Seventeen German divisions launched a great surprise attack in Belgium against the 12th US Army. After rolling over the American lines their goal was to cross the Maas and recapture the port of Antwerp in order to cut the Allied armies off from their source of supply and so prevent the invasion of Germany.

Two different pictures of the 6th Airborne Division in operation during the Battle of the Bulge. Above, on reconnaissance in the snowy landscape, these soldiers are coated with the snow camouflage suit which were given out in December 1944. The soldier at left is a sniper, armed with the telescopic sight No. 4T. (photo IWM).

Below, Canadian paratroopers on patrol in a ruined village in the Ardennes. (photo PAC)

Carefully prepared, the German offensive began with a massive artillery bombardment that paved the way for the advance of two great armoured formations. According to the plan, the 6th SS Panzer Army to the north under Sepp Dietrich was to cross the River Maas in the area of Liège and then take Antwerp. To the south, Hasso von Manteuffel's 5th Panzer Army would cross the Maas at Namur and press on to capture Brussels. The 7th Army would follow as a covering force. The success of the plan would result in the encirclement and annihilation of the Anglo-Canadian 21st Army Group and likely put an end to any possibility of an invasion of German territory from the west. The zone selected for the attack and the sheer force of the opening assault took the Americans completely by surprise. The Americans, fewer in number, were overrun in many places, yet resisted firmly enough to slow the enemy's progress and keep the Germans from gaining all their first-day objectives. The US high command tried to get a clear sense of the scale of the German offensive, but the reports coming back from the battle zone were very confusing. To make matters worse, the poor weather conditions ruled out support or reconnaissance from the Allied air forces until December 24th. Nevertheless, the 7th and 10th US Armoured Divisions were sent as reinforcements on the night of December 16th-17th. The same night, roughly eight hundred German paratroopers, commanded by Oberstleutnant Von Der Heydte, were dropped in a bid to seize the road junction at Mont Rigi and thus enable the armoured columns to push through to Liège. The wide scattering of the paratroopers was the undoing of their plan, however, and they were slowly but surely rounded up as prisoners of war over the next few days. At the same time, special troops under the notorious SS-Obersturmbannführer Otto Skorzeny, equipped with American uniforms and vehicles, sowed confusion and carried out sabotage operations in the American lines – They also started a real obsession of the undercover among Americans. On the evening of December 17th, the 82nd and 101st US Airborne Divisions were also despatched to the front but with little or no equipment for winter warfare in the Ardennes. Yet both of these famous units distinguished themselves, most memorably at La Gleize and Bastogne. The penetration made by the German forces took the shape of a wedge with its point aimed at Dinant. This wedge split the 12th US Army Group into two parts and prevented General Omar Bradley from taking effective control of the American forces in the north. As a result, on December 20th, General Eisenhower gave Field Marshal Montgomery command of all Allied forces north of the enemy salient (the "Bulge"), namely, the British 21st Army Group and 1st and 9th US Armies. Montgomery, who had begun to place units between Liège and Dinant on December 19th, had 30th British Corps move down from the north.

In sheer desperation, US and British paratroopers plug the gaps.

The 6th Airborne as reinforcements

The 30th Corps wielded three independent armoured brigades, the Guards Armoured Division, and three infanty divisions (51st Highland, 53rd Welsh, 43rd Wessex) and was at first concentrated between Louvain and St-Trond, then in defence along the Meuse. In Britain, the 6th Airborne Division, reinforced and refitted after the losses in Normandy, was training vigorously for urban warfare and river crossings in anticipation of future operations on the Rhine. The division, however, also made up part of the Allies' strategic reserve and in this capacity received orders on December 20th to deploy to Belgium. It left its quarters in Wiltshire and embarked for Ostend; it was an emergency operation and an airborne deployment was not thought possible. The better part of the division spent Christmas Eve at Ostend, and over the next two days took up positions between Dinant and Namur under the command of 30th British Corps. By placing his troops in this area, Montgomery hoped to take the pressure off 7th US Corps so as to allow it to focus its efforts in the direction of Houffalize. He also hoped that General George Patton's 3rd Army could move up from the south to join hands with the 30th Corps and thus cut the head off the German salient. The furthest point of this salient was blunted by an attack carried out the by 6th Airborne.

The 5th Parachute Brigade advanced on the right towards Grupont and the 3rd towards Rochefort. The Germans put up stubborn resistance, with the 5th Brigade encountering the most tenacious defence. To ease the task of taking Grupont, it was decided that the village of Bure should be captured first. This objective was assigned to the 13th Battalion, with armoured support from the tanks of the Fife & Forfar Yeomanry and additional infantry from 'C' Company of the Ox & Bucks. The attack went in on January 3rd, 1945, in intense cold and snowdrifts that made movement extremely difficult. The assault on the village was a costly affair, so much so that Major Jack Watson, commanding 'A' Company, reported that he had lost a third of his men. Only a part of Bure was captured, however, and the paratroopers had to stand their ground against ferocious German counterattacks. These attacks were supported by Panzers that shot to pieces many of the Shermans of the Fife & Forfar Yeomanry fighting alongside the paratroopers.

Two days later the Germans made no less than five attempts to recapture Bure, but this time the paratroopers had the close support of the 25-pounders and 5.5" guns of the Royal Artillery and the attacks were repulsed. The German artillery took a turn trying to pulverise the village but did not inflict much harm on the paratroopers who were by now used to

Two paratroop radio operators at Helden, February 3rd, 1945.
(photo © IWM)

these bombardments from their experience in Normandy. A new attack then ensued, with two Panzers adding their weight, but this attack, too, was contained and the British set about clearing the portion of Bure held by the enemy. The capture of the village was finally achieved after savage fighting, often in close, hand to hand combat with edged weapons.

By 21h00 on January 5th, Bure was entirely in the hands of the paratroopers. The 7th Battalion had by the same time completed the capture of Grupont. In the battle for Bure, the 13th Battalion lost 189 men, of whom sixty-eight were killed, while 'C' Company of the Ox & Bucks mourned the loss of twenty-one men. Sixteen Shermans of the Fife & Forfar Yeomanry had been destroyed. On January 28th, 1945, the Battle of the Bulge ended, twelve days after the American 1st and 3rd Armies succeeded in linking up at Houffalize. The determined resistance of American soldiers in the initial stages of the offensive and the energetic counterattacks afterwards which they carried out in cooperation with the British put an end to the last German offensive in western Europe. American losses rose as high as 75,522; the British lost 1,400 soldiers, and the Germans 67,675 – unlike those of the Allies, however, the German losses in men and materiel could not be replaced. At the end of January, the 6th Airborne Division was sent to the Netherlands, between the towns of Venlo and Roermond along the Meuse, where it faced the German 7th Parachute Division. The British units were responsible for patrolling and reconnaissance in this sector where the terrain was particularly difficult, both liberally sown with mines and flooded by the Germans who opened the dam on the Roer river. To do their patrolling, the paratroopers had to cross an unusually wide Maas which was running high with a strong current. From their sector the paratroopers made many incursions into the enemy lines, identifying positions and marking targets for the artillery.

On February 13th, 1st Canadian Army completed the capture of the Reichswald Forest area and came within sight of the Rhine. A few days later, the 6th Airborne Division returned to England to prepare for the decisive blow – the invasion of Germany.

Below, three Canadian paratroopers in the Ardennes. (photo NARA).
Below, signallers of the 6th Airborne Division in Holland in January 1945. (photo PAC)

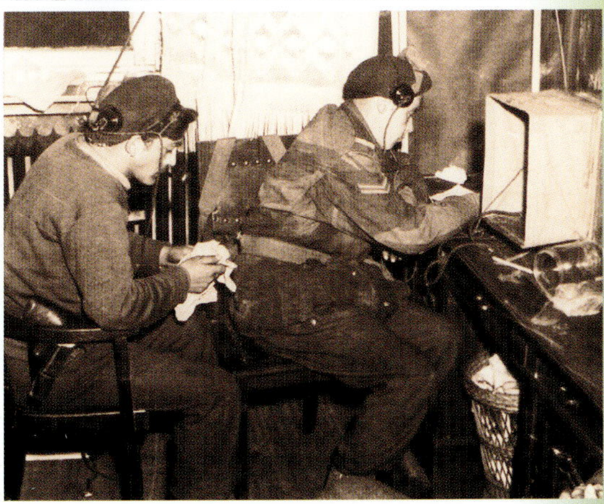

At the Elbe River in April 1945, Field Marshal Montgomery (centre) poses with some officers of the 6th Airborne. Major Watson stands two to the left of Monty. (photo © IWM)

Jack Watson during a commemorative ceremony at Ranville.

Major Jack Watson's Military Cross

At Bure, on January 3rd, 1945, Major Watson was leading 'A' Company of the 13th Battalion. By the time the assault began, the German mortars had already inflicted twenty-eight casualties. Watson's paratroopers hit the enemy hard and drove back an attack by Tiger tanks by using their PIATs. The major made skilful use of these weapons and did not hesitate to lure a Tiger towards himself so that his men could take careful aim at the target.

In January 1945, somewhere in the Ardennes, a patrol from the 9th Parachute Battalion moves forward under enemy mortar fire. (photo © IWM)

© The objects shown on these pages come from the collections of the Pegasus Memorial in Ranville.

Major Watson's medals, from left to right: Military Cross, 1939-45 Star, France-Germany Star, Defence Medal, 1939-45 War Medal, General Service Medal (with a bar for "Palestine 1948"), and the Légion d'Honneur (France).

On December 24th, 1944, in the village of Bande, a detachment of the SS security branch (the Sicherheitsdienst) executed thirty-four Belgian civilians. The bodies were discovered on January 11th, 1945, by the 1st Canadian Parachute Battalion. When it relieved the Canadians, the 9th Parachute Battalion held a respectful funeral service for the victims of this atrocity. (photo © IWM)

This figurine was made from the plywood of a glider by Lance-Corporal W.H. Short, 'C' Company, 2nd Ox & Bucks. Short won the Military Medal on August 25th at Manneville-la-Raoult, but was to be killed in action in Bure on January 6th, 1945.

On this silk escape map, the sector where the 6th Airborne intervened in the Battle of the Bulge can be seen, notably the village of Bande where the paratroopers of the 9th Battalion honoured the 34 civilians massacred by the Nazis.

T
272692

In one of the landing zones, a Bren carrier and a motorcycle from the 6th Airborne Division pass in front of a Hamilcar with its nose section open, having already disgorged its cargo. (photo © IWM)

A lieutenant and a sergeant from the 1st Canadian Parachute Battalion bow their heads at the grave of their commanding officer, Lieutenant-Colonel Jeff Nicklin. (photo PAC)

Operation Varsity

From the Rhine to the Baltic, March 24th-May 1st, 1945

On March 23rd, 1945, Montgomery sent 21st Army Group and 9th US Army into the assault on Germany. The next day, in mid-morning, the last great airborne operation of the Second World War got underway: the 17th US Airborne Division and the 6th British Airborne Division jumped east of the Rhine, near Wesel, to establish a bridgehead in advance of the land forces.

Allied bombers and artillery hammered the German positions along the Rhine all through March 22nd and 23rd. On the evening of the 23rd, the 79th US Infantry Division and the 1st Special Service Brigade crossed the river. The 15th Scottish Infantry Division followed the next morning. In front of the Scottish division and the commando brigade were the wooded heights of the Diersfordterwald, northwest of the town of Wesel. The US and British airborne divisions had to take control of this feature and forestall any German counterattacks. The British paratroopers had the specific task of capturing three bridges over the Issel River and the village of Hamminkeln. Every precaution had been taken so as not to repeat the disaster at Arnhem where the 1st Airborne Division had been handicapped from the outset as a result of being dropped in several waves into Drop Zones that were too far from the objectives. This time, in the operation christened Varsity, 21,680 British and Americans would land by parachute or on board 1,348 gliders in one wave coming directly onto the objectives. Furthermore, the frequencies for sending radio signals would be strong enough to maintain contact with air and artillery at any given moment. The presence of a great many German anti-aircraft units had been noted in the areas around the intended drop zones. Therefore, half an hour before the first landings, the artillery of 2nd British Army unleashed a tremendous barrage: eleven field regiments, the same number of medium regiments, and even several heavy artillery units pounded the sector. Despite this, however, the majority of the German anti-aircraft guns were still operational and would inflict heavy losses. In Drop Zone 'A' the bulk of the 3rd Parachute Brigade was preceded by the 8th Parachute Battalion which was to secure the area. It was bad luck that this zone remained under fire from German machine gunners and riflemen who targeted the paratroopers as they came down or tried to free themselves when they were ensnarled in branches. Not a few of the men killed were left hanging in the trees, suspended by the parachute cords; one of them was Lieutenant-Colonel Jeff Nicklin, commander of the 1st Canadian Parachute Battalion. Despite the loss of their commander, the Canadians took control of the two crossroads on the Wesel-Rees road which had been set as their objectives. The heights overlooking this road were soon in the hands of the 9th Parachute Battalion which took out an enemy artillery position and captured 293 prisoners. The 8th Battalion spent part of the day protecting DZ A before placing itself in protection of the divsional command post between Landing Zone P and Drop Zone A. But Drop Zone B was contested even more bitterly than DZ A. An enemy 88 mm anti-aircraft gun fired into the paratroopers of 5th Brigade as they drifted down.

For the paras, the campaign in Germany would be far more costly than Normandy.

Photographed from a Stirling bomber, these Horsa gliders would soon be crossing the frontier of the Reich itself. (photo © IWM)

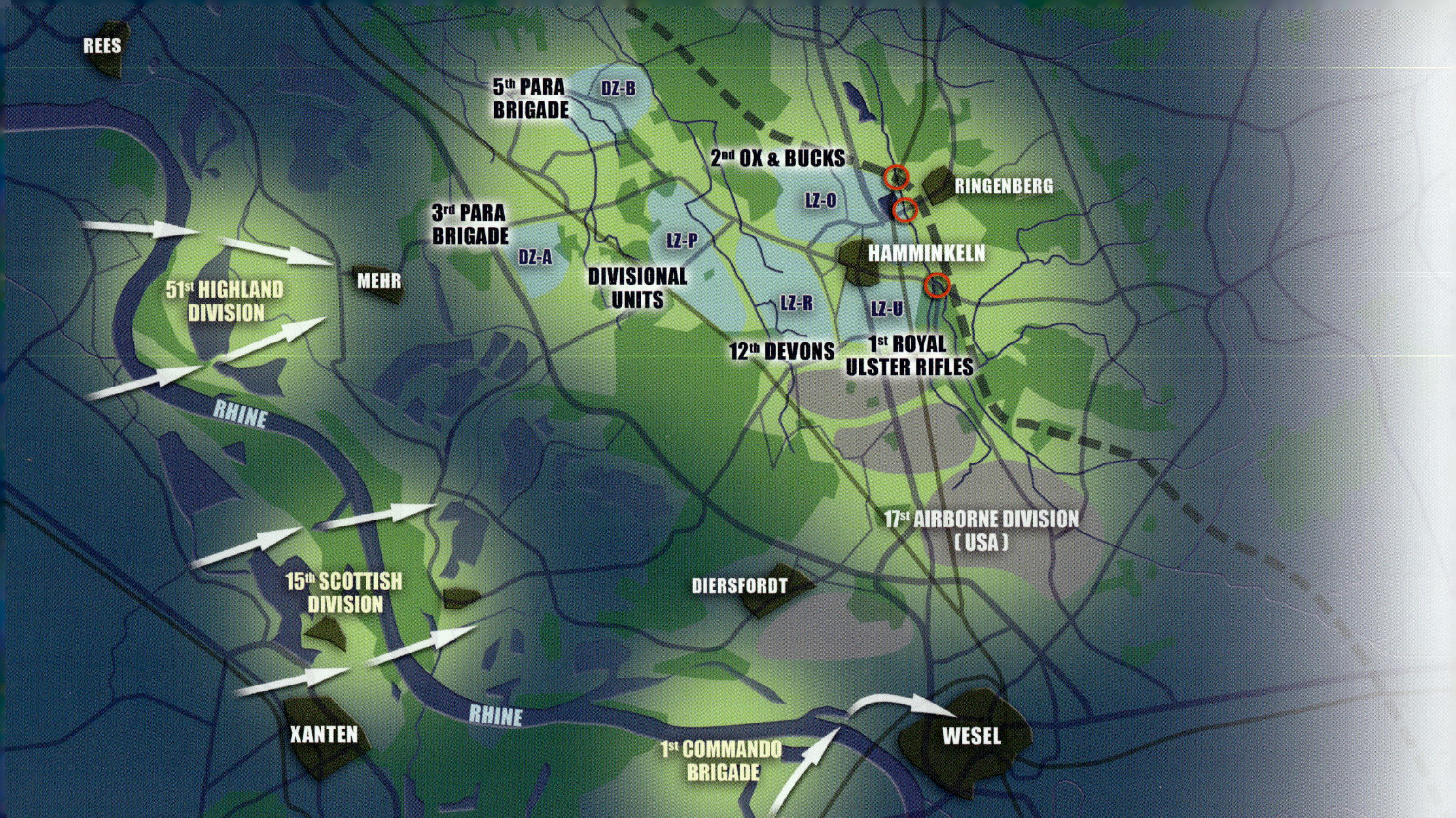

The Rhine crossing

The German gun crews were finally captured by the 12th Battalion. The 13th Battalion likewise descended under fire from the Flak, landing a little too far to the east of the intended zone because of the dense smoke caused by the preliminary barrage.

The glider-borne units, including the 6th Airlanding Brigade, support troops, and a part of the mortars from the Parachute Battalions, would suffer greatly from anti-aircraft fire. Many gliders were hit while in flight and a number were set on fire, leaving no survivors. In Landing Zone O, north of Hamminkeln, the 2nd Ox & Bucks took heavy casualties, all within ten minutes of landing. By day's end the unit had lost over half its men, including 103 killed.

Eight Locust tanks from the 6th Airborne Armoured Reconnaissance Regiment had been loaded onto Hamilcar gliders for Operation Varsity. Only four would reach their rendezvous point and two others would be destroyed before nightfall. Twenty-two of the 78 gliders headed for Landing Zone P were lost and many others could not put down in the right place. As a result, the 53rd Worcestershire Yeomanry could use only half its intended firepower. Making matters worse, the 2nd Airlanding Anti-Tank Regiment could locate only a dozen of the thirty-two guns it was supposed to have. To top it all off, because of the intense anti-aircraft fire and the poor visibility, the Americans of the 513th Parachute Infantry Regiment were scattered far and wide across the landing zones assigned to the 6th Airlanding Brigade.

This flag was claimed as a trophy in May 1945 by Sapper Harry Mosley who found it in a townhall near Wismar.

Emerging out of the confusion of the first few moments, they gave effective support to the British airborne soldiers. Despite their losses, the 2nd Ox & Bucks succeeded in knocking out the anti-aircraft batteries in its sector and by late morning had taken the two bridges over the Issel designated as their objectives. In Landing Zone U, the Royal Ulster Rifles who had also come through anti-aircraft fire were under attack from tanks. They managed to destroy one of them and repel the others. The Irishmen then went on to capture their objectives, the third bridge over the Issel and the station at Hamminkeln, which they stoutly defended against enemy self-propelled guns. At the end of the day the Royal Ulster Rifles were holding firm around their perimeter; since mid-morning 259 Riflemen had been killed, wounded, or reported missing.

The 12th Devonshire Regiment came down in Landing Zone R in conditions similar to those in other sectors: thick smoke on the ground and murderous anti-aircraft fire. Under the leadership of their commander, Lieutenant-Colonel Paul Gleadell, the Devons regrouped and captured Hamminkeln by 13h00. Assisted by the 3rd Airlanding Anti-Tank Battery, they held out against German armour attacks but suffered from mortar fire and self-propelled guns throughout the day. The regiment lost 140 men that day, 27 of them killed.

By evening on March 24th, Operation Varsity could be considered as a tactical success. The 6th Airborne had taken and held all its objectives, and the land forces that had crossed the Rhine had succeeded in linking up. Even though dropped into chaotic conditions, the paratroopers of the 3rd and 5th Parachute Brigades had shown their effectiveness and their capacity for improvisation in organising themselves and winning control of the objectives, without suffering inordinate casualties. Unfortunately, the glider-borne troops were often trapped in their brittle plywood craft. These bulky targets without engines were riddled by anti-aircraft fire which set off explosions in the equipment and the gas tanks of vehicles carried on board. A hundred glider pilots lost their lives and the 6th Airlanding Brigade lost more soldiers on March 24th than it did during the entire Normandy campaign.

The Allied armies advanced rapidly after crossing the Rhine. The 6th Airborne blazed a trail across Germany that was punctuated by bouts of hard fighting, as at Lembeck on March 28th-29th. The drive ended at Wismar, on the shores of the Baltic, on May 2nd, 1945. It was then a matter of standing astride the route of the Red Army to keep it out of Denmark. The Soviets halted just before Wismar after a somewhat tense first encounter in which the Soviet commander declared his intention to pass through the town on the way to Lübeck, only to have the commander of the 6th Airborne Division, Major-General Eric Bols, reply that he had an airborne division and five artillery regiments which he would use if push came to shove. The situation was defused on May 7th, thanks to a meeting between Field-Marshal Montgomery and Marshal Rokossovsky. With this foretaste of the Cold War, the Second World War officially came to an end in Europe the next day. In the last six weeks of the fighting, the 6th Airborne had lost nearly 700 dead.

A Bren carrier of the 716th Light Company of the Royal Army Service Corps is loaded down with Devons in the streets of Hamminkeln, March 25th, 1945. (photo © IWM)

At Gleven, on April 5th, 1945, Captain Sid Mooney, who would win the Military Cross that day, and his counterpart, I.C. Stewart, both with the 2nd Forward Observation Unit. The two officers have shed their Denison smocks for "liberated" and much warmer German anoraks. (photo PAC)

2nd Forward Observation Unit, The "eyes" of the artillery

The airborne Forward Observation Units (FOU) had roughly a hundred men working in teams of four or five. These artillery observers were spread throughout each parachute or glider-borne battalion, and they came in with the first waves by parachute or by glider. They transmitted their firing instructions to the artillery the moment its support became necessary.

The 2nd Forward Observation Unit was officially created for the 6th Airborne Division on August 1st, 1944. The core of the unit was made up of artillery observers who had jumped with the division in Normandy. These men were gunners who volunteered for the paratroops and were rapidly qualified before the invasion. They were at that time placed under the command of the 53rd Airlanding Light Regiment.

The 2nd FOU included a command section, four sections of six teams each, and four liaison groups made up of Canadians. Every team had jeeps and the necessary radio apparatus. The 2nd FOU took part in the Ardennes battles and the operations at the River Maas. It distinguished itself in the Rhine crossing and in the race to the Baltic. Bombardier George Halewood won the Military Medal for continuing to send his instructions while under fire from a German 88 mm gun on March 25th, 1945; one of the twelve Canadian officers, Captain Sidney Arthur Mooney, was awarded the Military Cross for his actions during the crossing of the Weser on April 5th-6th, 1945. He was working at the time with the 2nd Ox & Bucks, and the firing instructions that he transmitted at the risk of his life allowed them to knock out a number of enemy positions during the river crossing and to crush a counterattack by Panzers the next day.

During the campaign in Germany, the 2nd FOU would suffer the loss of six men killed and fourteen wounded.

At Wismar, a White M3 Scout Car of the Red Army is surrounded by artillerymen of the 6th Airborne and a few American GIs. (photo PAC)

The beret of Captain H.H. Thompson 53rd Airlanding Light Regiment

A veteran of the Normandy campaign, Captain Thompson would be a victim of anti-aircraft fire during Operation Varsity. Captain Thompson, Sergeant Brackner, and Gunners Harvey, Gordon, Allingham, and Gore had taken their places in a Horsa Mark II, serial number 175F. The craft was also carrying a radio jeep with a trailer and two light motorcycles. The Horsa touched down in Landing Zone P after being hit by anti-aircraft fire. Captain Thompson and Gunner Allingham were wounded, and one of the motorcycles was put out of use, but the other motorcycle and the jeep exited without difficulty through the hinged nose section.

Beret with bullion badge worn by Captain Thompson.

At least for the photo, cordial relations have been restored between this Canadian paratrooper and a Soviet officer who are symbolically shaking hands across a barrier delimiting their respective sectors. (photo PAC)

The same Soviet officer poses with Gunner H.V. Mellenger of the 2nd FOU. For some reason Mellenger is wearing an American belt with a Colt .45 holster from which protrudes the butt of a Luger, no doubt a souvenir of the war... (photo PAC)

© The objects shown on these pages come from the collections of the Pegasus Memorial in Ranville.

Three recruits in the summer of 1944 whose faces show how achingly young they were. Tom Markey is on the right.

Rifleman Tom Markey

18 years of age, 8 months of service

In August of 1944, Tom Markey quit his job carding wool at the Albert Works at Whitewell Bottom in Lancashire to join the army. He entered the ranks of the 1st Battalion, The Royal Ulster Rifles, part of the 6th Airborne Division. On March 24th, 1945, the young Rifleman took part in the airborne assault on Germany alongside his comrades, many of them veterans of Normandy. A week later, on March 31st, the war diary of the 1st Royal Ulsters briefly noted the loss of nine men in the advance on Greven. Tom Markey was one of them. He now lies at rest in the large Commonwealth War Cemetery in the Reichswald Forest.

AFTER EIGHT MONTHS

WHITEWELL BOTTOM SOLDIER KILLED.

Pte. Tom Markey, who as briefly reported in last Saturday's "Free Press," has been killed in action in Western Europe. He was the son of Mr. and Mrs. Stanley Markey, 1, Fountain, Whitewell Bottom, and joined the Forces only in August last. He was 18½ years of age, and in civil life was employed in the cardroom of the Albert Works, Whitewell Bottom.

Tom Markey's death in action announced in his local newspaper.

This press clipping showing airborne troops was saved along with his effects by Tom Markey's next of kin.

Tom Markey's medals

Left to right, 1939-45 Star, for 180 days in an area of operations or participation in a specific operation; France-Germany Star, for participation in the campaign in northwest Europe between June 6th, 1944, and May 8th, 1945. War Medal 1939-45, for 28 days service in an area of operations. These decorations were common to all soldiers who fought in Europe. The ones shown were bestowed posthumously and from their pristine condition we can see that they were never worn.

Two Royal Ulsters at the beginning of the campaign in Germany, posing by the roadsign announcing entry into Hamminkeln, in March 1945. (photo © IWM)

Whitewell Bottom. Tom Markey grew up in this Lancashire town with its many mills. The mill where he worked until he enlisted is shown in the foreground.

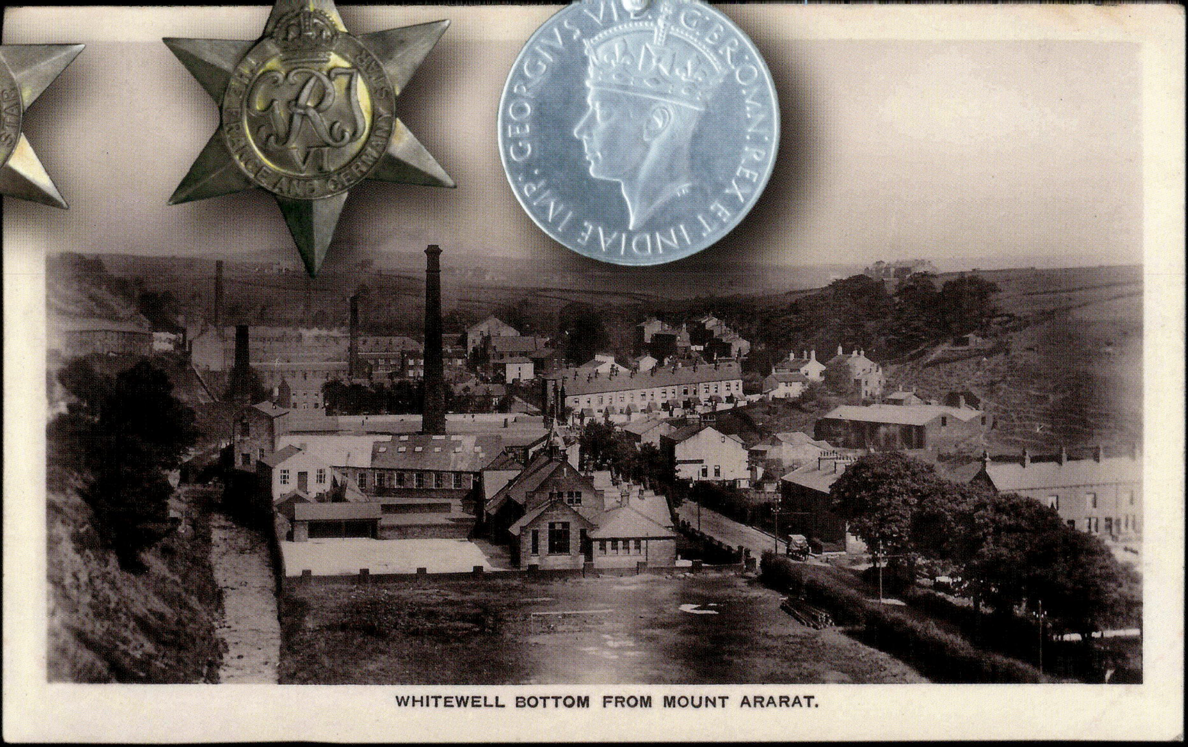

Germany, 1945. Sappers from the 3rd Parachute Squadron posent with their war trophy. Fred Singleton, standing, second row, is indicated by an 'x'. The second standing man from the left is Lieutenant Wade who led a reconnaissance patrol to the bridge at Troarn on the morning of June 6th.

Sapper Fred Singleton, during his time in the Far East, 1945-46.

Sapper Fred Singleton

From Normandy to the Far East

Sapper Fred Singleton parachuted into Normandy on the night of June 5th-6th, 1944, with the 3rd Parachute Squadron. During this and his other campaigns (Ardennes, Germany, Asia) he collected souvenirs that he kept all his life.
These objects, bits and pieces in his personal "kit," German and Japanese trophies, retrace the path of a soldier.

Laid out on Fred Singleton's camouflage netting are his field service knife and beret which he kept and wore during his pilgrimages to Normandy; a poppy from one of these journeys has been tucked behind the cap badge.

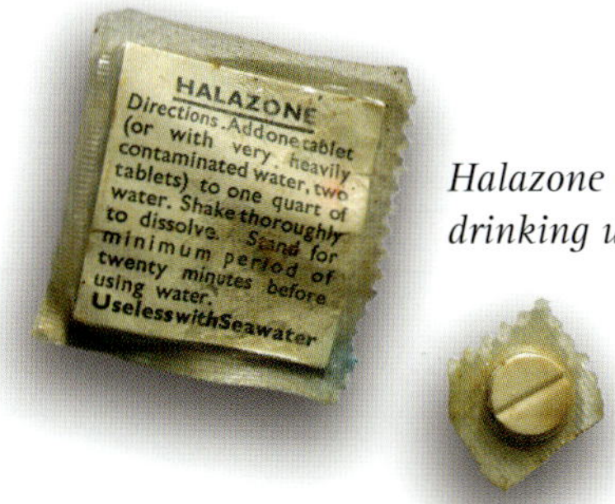

Halazone tablets to purify drinking water.

Several German war trophies: placed on this Wehrmacht athletic jersey are a campaign medal from the Eastern Front (left), a badge given to men wounded in 1914-18, and a braided cord worn by a sharpshooter in the German Army. Below, two "pips" indicating rank.

A trinket, or good-luck charm, made of two bullets from a Lee-Enfield rifle.

© The objects shown on these pages come from the collections of the Pegasus Memorial in Ranville.

Some Japanese trophies: a small book, a cigarette lighter, and a petty officer's epaulette from the Japanese Imperial Navy.

Corporal Topham being filmed by the Army Film & Photo Unit after receiving the Victoria Cross.
(photo PAC)

Corporal George Topham

The Victoria Cross winner of the 6th Airborne Division

A medical orderly in the 1st Canadian Parachute Battalion, George Topham was born in Toronto on August 10th, 1917. On March 24th, 1945, during Operation Varsity, he was parachuted into Drop Zone A. At about 11h00 he went to the aid of a wounded man lying out in the open; beside him were two men from the 224th Field Ambulance who had just been killed. After reaching the soldier Topham was tending to his wounds when he himself became a target and took a bullet through the nose.

Without allowing himself to be affected by the flow of blood running over him or by the pain of his own wound, he devoted his attention to the wounded man whom he succeeded in bringing to safety. In the two hours that followed, Corporal Topham refused all aid and continued to assist other soldiers while under fire from the enemy. The medical orderly did not allow himself to be treated until the last of his patients had been looked after. When orders came for his immediate evacuation, he refused outright and returned to join his company. On the way he came upon a scene full of horror: three soldiers were trapped in a Bren Carrier set on fire by a German mortar bomb. The ammunition was beginning to explode and German mortar shells were still falling all around. A British officer gave the order not to approach the vehicle. Topham paid no attention but crossed the open ground between him and the flaming wreckage. Without concern for the explosions he was able to pull the three men out of the inferno. Two of them survived thanks to the courageous medical orderly. For his courage, Corporal Topham received the Victoria Cross in August 1945.

At left, Corporal George Topham, of Toronto, Ontario, Canada.

At right, with the crimson ribbon of the Victoria Cross on his blouse, Corporal Topham displays a war trophy brought back from Germany.
(photos PAC)

Framed plaque commemorating Corporal Topham at the Pegasus Memorial.

Brigadier James Hill's beret, with the rank insignia worn after 1952.

This cane was an inseparable part of Brigadier Hill's image. He carried it all the way from Tunisia to Germany by way of Normandy and the Ardennes.

Brigadier Hill's collar patches.

© The objects shown on these pages come from the collections of the Pegasus Memorial in Ranville.

Major-General Matthew Ridgway, commander of the 18th US Airborne Corps, confers the Silver Star on Brigadier Hill after the crossing of the Rhine in March 1945. (document Pegasus Memorial / DR)

Statue of Brigadier Hill at the Pegasus Memorial.

An affectionate caricature of "Speedy" Hill done in 1931 when he was serving with the Royal Fusiliers.

Brigadier James Hill, DSO, MC

Born in 1911, Hill entered the Royal Military College at Sandhurst in 1929. There he gained the nickname "Speedy" because of his athletic talents. A veteran of the BEF and Dunkirk, and among the first to volunteer for the paratroopers, he was a charismatic leader whose human qualities and sense of humour made him very popular. In 1942, he distinguished himself in action with his 1st Parachute Battalion in Tunisia where he was badly wounded but won the Distinguished Service Order. After promotion to Brigadier, Hill commanded the 3rd Parachute Brigade in Normandy, and afterwards in the Ardennes and in Germany. He received a bar to his DSO, the Military Cross, the Légion d'Honneur (France), the Silver Star (USA), and King Haakon VII's Cross of Freedom (Norway). *(photo © IWM)*

The brigadiers of D-Day Hill, Poett and Kindersley

Brigadier Nigell Poett, KCB, DSO

Nigel Poett was born in 1907. The son of a high-ranking officer, he quickly decided on a military career. Upon graduation from Sandhurst in 1927, he served in Egypt, India, and the Sudan. When the Second World War broke out, he was posted to the War Office to work on the allocation of weapons.. He obtained a command in France but found himself back at the War Office after the evacuation at Dunkirk. He commanded the 11th Battalion, Durham Light Infantry, in 1943, before taking command of the 5th Parachute Brigade. He straightway qualified as a paratrooper and jumped with the advance elements on June 6th. He was awarded the DSO for his actions in Normandy and received a bar to this award after the Rhine crossing. *(photo © IWM)*

Brigadier Hugh Kindersley, CBE, MC

Born in 1889, Hugh Kindersley was the son of the first Baron Kindersley. He fought in France in 1917-18 as an officer in the Scots Guards, and won the Military Cross. At the beginning of the Second World War, he was in command of an armoured battalion of the Scot Guards. He was promoted to Brigadier in 1943, and the same year, he took charge of the 6th Airlanding Brigade. Kindersley was qualified both as a glider pilot and as a paratrooper, and he was the one who recommended John Howard's company for the assault on the bridges at Bénouville and Ranville. He arrived at Ranville with the first wave of gliders in the predawn hours of June 6th. Unfortunately, he was seriously wounded a few days later, on June 12th, at the same time as Lord Lovat. *(photo © IWM)*

Orders and decorations of Sir Richard Gale. At left, the sash badge and breast star of Knight Grand Cross of the Most Honourable Order of th Bath ; above these is the insignia of Commandeur de la Légion d'Honneur (France) ; centre, the neck badge of Commander of the Legion of Merit (USA). On the right, from top to bottom, insignia of Grand Officier de l'Ordre de la Couronne (Belgium); insignia of Commander of the Most Excellent Order of the British Empire. In the row of medals below the photograph, the Distinguished Service Order can be seen at the far left. (Collection of the Mercian (Worcestershire) Regiment Museum)

Major-General Richard N. Gale
GCB, KBE, DSO, MC

In command of 6th Airborne Division from its inception, Major-General Richard Nelson Gale was a seasoned officer who had survived the horrors of battle in the Great War. Gale quickly grasped the tactical possibilities which the new airborne arm offered and sought to make full use of them. He was also very concerned to preserve his soldiers' lives. He was a very popular figure among his men, and he led with calm deliberation and efficiency.

Born in London on July 25th, 1896, Richard Gale spent his first ten years in Australia and New Zealand. Although of a literary and imaginative cast of mind, he hardly blossomed at school and later defined himself as a student who belonged in the category of "could do better if he tried." He showed early on his desire to become an officer but his school results got in his way. He therefore quit school at the age of seventeen to take up, without much enthusiasm, a career in the City. He tried to enlist in August of 1914 but his frail physical condition kept him from being accepted. A year of athletic training helped to solve that problem, and in 1915 he entered the Royal Military College at Sandhurst. He went to France as a lieutenant with the 164th Machine Gun Company and took part in the Battle of the Somme, later seeing action in the Ypres Salient and at Messines Ridge. He escaped death miraculously a number of times, but the terrible fate of the men who fell at his side deeply affected him. His CO gave him leave to recuperate from his mental and physical exhaustion. He returned to the front in January of 1918 to serve with the 126th Machine Gun Company. During the German offensive on the Somme in March of 1918, Gale and his men, though surrounded, succeeded in regaining their own lines where their machine guns played a key role in halting the enemy advance. At the end of the war Captain Gale carried on his military career in India with the Machine Gun Corps, then with the infantry when the MG Corps was dissolved in 1921. From 1938 to 1941 he served on the General Staff and was delighted to leave when offered command of an infantry regiment. In September 1941 he was entrusted with the formation and command of the 1st Parachute Brigade. He worked on perfecting the airborne arm developed by his immediate superior, Major-General Frederick Browning, by choosing officers capable of taking tactical initiatives once on the ground and by reducing the rate of accidents in training jumps. It was Gale who selected Major John Frost for the raid on Bruneval on February 27th, 1942, but he was to be disappointed when his brigade was sent to North Africa without him, as he had been assigned to the War Office to help foster cooperation between the Army and the RAF in airborne warfare. On May 3rd, 1943, Gale was promoted to Major-General and given command of the newly formed 6th Airborne Division. From this point on he dedicated all his energy to making it into an elite formation, ready for the invasion. On February 17th, 1944, he learned that his division would be at the head of the forces carrying out the landings, and with his staff he ironed out each phase of his troops' assault. On the night of D-Day he was to lead his men in person on the ground.

Sir Richard "Windy" Gale. The commander of the 6th Airborne Division wears a Windak Smock, a more "upscale" jump vest favoured by high-ranking officers. (photo © IWM)

As he boarded his Horsa glider (no. 70), Major-General Gale was offered by way of a parting gift a can of treacle by Group Captain Wilfred Surplice, station commander at RAF Harwell. Gale had mentioned his fondness for this delicacy and was deeply touched by the gesture. (photo © IWM)

Major-General Gale in front of his command post at Bas-de-Ranville, decorated with a pennant of the 6th Airborne Division. (photo © IWM)

However, during a later visit, Browning chided him for the placement of his command post at Bas-le-Ranville, which he thought was a little too close to the enemy for his taste. For his conduct of the fighting at Breville, Gale received the DSO. He succeeded Browning at the head of 1st British Airborne Corps and 1st Allied Airborne Army in December of 1944. His performance in this role during the invasion of Germany earned him the American Legion of Merit and appointment to Companion of the Most Honourable Order of the Bath. At the end of the European war, Gale left for Asia and planned for the capture of Bangkok by the 6th Airborne and the 44th Indian Airborne Division, an operation called off when the Japanese surrendered.

In 1946-47 Gale commanded the 1st Infantry Division in Egypt and Palestine and at the end of 1947 regained his wartime rank of Lieutenant-General, this time to command the British forces in the Mediterranean area (with the exception of Malta and Gibraltar). He then became director of military training at the War Office in 1949, serving until 1952. He was knighted during this period, and then took up command of the British Army of the Rhine in Germany from 1952 to 1957, also serving as Queen Elizabeth II's aide-de-camp from 1954 to 1957. He tried to retire from the army in 1957 but was recalled to serve as Deputy Supreme Commander of the allied forces within NATO. He retired from the army for good in 1960.

Sir Richard Gale's original beret, presented to the Pegasus Memorial. It is the standard model made by Kangol Wear Ltd.

This medal of an Officer of the Legion of Merit was conferred upon Major-General Gale by the American general Omar Bradley in 1944. Gale was afterwards elevated to the rank of Commander; the neck badge can be seen on his uniform shown opposite.

Sir Richard Gale's service dress and personal effects. The ribbons of British, American, and French decorations from two world wars are sewn over the left breast pocket.

Major-General Gale addresses a last few words to his Red Berets, the vanguard of the invasion that would restore freedom to the peoples of western Europe.
(photo © IWM)

Bibliography

BOOKS

- Ambrose, Stephen E., « Pegasus Bridge, 6 juin 1944 », France horizon 1987.
- Bouchery, Jean, « Le Tommy de la Libération » tome 1 et 2, Histoire et Collections 1998-1999.
- Chappell, Mike, « The British soldier in the 20th century », n°10
- Chappell, Mike, « Airborne Uniforms » Wessex Military Publishing 1990
- Chant, Christopher, « Operation Overlord, Sword Beach & The British 6th Airborne Division 6 June 1944 », Ravelin 1994.
- Chion, Thierry, « Le prix à payer », Petit à Petit 2001.
- Crookenden, Napier, « Les paras du 6 juin », Albin Michel 1994.
- Edwards, Denis, « The devil's own luck », Leo Cooper, London 1999.
- Florentin, Eddy, « Opération Paddle », Presses de la Cité 1983.
- Golley, John, « La nuit des canons de Merville », Presses de la Cité 1983.
- Davis, Brian L. « British Army Uniforms & Insignia of World War Two », Arms and Armour Press 1983.
- Fisher, Daniel et Lock, Oliver, « British Airborne Headdress », Military Mode Publishing in collaboration with The Airborne Assault Museum. 2014
- Harclerode, Peter, « Go to it ! », Caxton Editions, London 2000.
- Horn, Bernd et Wyczynski, Michel, « Tip of the spear », The Dundurn Group, Toronto 2002.
- Howarth, David, « 6 juin à l'aube », Presses de la Cité 1959.
- Millin, Bill, Piper, « Invasion », The Book Guild Limited, Lewes, Sussex, 1991.
- Montgomery, Field Marshal, « Normandy to the Baltic », Hutchinson & Co. Ltd 1946.
- Pine-Coffin, R.G. et Maddox, Barbara, « The tale of two bridges », Published by Peter Pine-Coffin 2003.
- Rambaud, Marthe, et Bosquain, Jean-Claude, « Gonneville-sur-mer 1939-1944 », 1995.
- Richard, Olivier, « Paras britanniques » E.T.A.I. 2010
- Richard, Olivier, « 1944, Les Canadiens en Normandie, de Juno Beach à Dieppe », De Rameau, 2013
- Shannon, Kevin et Wright, Stephen, « One night in June », Airlife Publishing Ltd, Shrewsbury 1994.
- Toupin, Christian et Grente, Samuel « La libération de Beuzeville et sa région » Municipalité de Beuzeville.
- Wilson, Bruce, in collaboration with Airborne Assault Museum & Military Mode Publishing « Denison, British airborne specialist clothing from WW2 to the present day » 2013.

MAGAZINES

- Bernage, Georges, « La nuit des paras », Historica N° 70, janvier-février-mars 2002.
- Bernage, Georges, « Les paras du Jour J », Historica N° 71, avril-mai-juin 2002.

Index